# POSITIVE
☑ ## PLUS

## The Practical Plan for Liking Yourself Better

# DR. JOYCE BROTHERS

G. P. Putnam's Sons • NEW YORK

G. P. Putnam's Sons
*Publishers Since 1838*
200 Madison Avenue
New York, NY 10016

ISBN 0-399-13937-0

Printed in the United States of America

*For my much adored daughter, Lisa, and her husband, Amir, who is the son I never had. You both make me so proud.*

# Author's Note

Although many of the examples in this book are female, and the use of "she" and "her" prevalent, much of the advice is applicable and helpful to men as well.

# CONTENTS

*Part One*

# ☑ SECOND CHANCES

*Chapter One*

# THE PERSON YOU WOULD LIKE TO BE

---

## How to Be Happier and More Successful

---

IS YOUR LIFE not what you hoped it would be? Do you feel that the love and warmth you expected in marriage, the stimulation you expected to find in your job, and the satisfaction of raising a family are all less than you hoped for? You are not alone.

It is easy to get off track these days. Life is complicated. Full of stress and anxiety. Our work, our families, our love relationships all make demands on us. We feel so pressured that many of us cheat ourselves. We don't give ourselves time to think, to get a perspective on ourselves and our lives, to ask "How am I doing?"

And that is a big mistake. Life does not need to be this way. You can change it. You can have the love, the stimulation and the joy you crave. You can give yourself a second chance in life. And you can start today. Just take a little time out for yourself right now and find out just how you are doing. Ask yourself:

Am I on the right track?
Am I making the most of myself?
Am I getting what I want out of life?
Am I happy?

If you answer "No" to even one of these questions, then it is no wonder you are walking around feeling overstressed and vaguely unhappy most of the time. You are getting a bum deal out of life.

I have learned in my years as a psychologist to literally hundreds of thousands of people through radio and television, columns and books, lectures and seminars and in my role as a corporate adviser that 99 percent of the people who feel this way can usually turn their lives around by making just one or two small changes in their attitudes or behavior. Just as one bad apple can spoil the whole barrel, one self-defeating trait may be holding you back from love and happiness and success, from the life you should be enjoying.

No one is perfect. Every single one of us from the president of the United States to the surly cashier at the supermarket checkout counters has self-defeating traits or behaviors. They are like invisible walls that stand between us and the life we want. I certainly have had my share, and in the course of this book I'll tell you how I dealt with some of them.

Most of us are all too aware of these self-defeating traits. We know we are too lazy or too critical, too abrasive or too shy. We worry too much or nag too often. We go on binges and spend ourselves into credit-card debt. We tell too many white lies. We're too gossipy, too nosy, too ingratiating. We're inhibited in bed. Some of us just can't say no. And like the song, others persist in looking for love in all the wrong places. The list is endless.

Almost everyone would like to be better. But how? How many New Year's resolutions have you broken? How many times have you promised yourself to straighten up and fly right, and stop yelling at the kids, and stick to a budget, and lose fifteen pounds, and be nicer to your sister-in-law? Why set yourself up for one more defeat?

Ah, but why not set yourself up for success?

You don't have to be perfect. That is impossible. But you can change. The secret of effective change is not a total psychological makeover. It is more a matter of tinkering with the trait or behavior that is sabotaging you. It may be tamping down your hot temper, curbing your impetuosity or reining in your bossiness. All you have to do is tune up or tune down that unwanted behavior, whatever it is, so that it's within the norm. And then, chances are, you will have turned it into an asset.

Turn a self-defeating trait into an asset? "Impossible!" you say. Not at all. Take yelling at the kids, for instance. If you are forever screaming at them like a fishwife, they stop paying attention. To them, it is just so much meaningless static. All that happens is that you become increasingly frustrated and angry.

But if you yell at them only once a month, just watch them jump to attention and pick up their room or stop fighting over whose turn it is to set the table. And you will feel good, because your shock treatment got results. You turned your yelling into an asset, an effective way of getting action.

Most self-defeating behaviors are like this. They can be fine-tuned into assets. Almost all negative attributes have a positive side. By modifying your undesirable trait, you can change your life so that in time you will find yourself back on the right track.


This book is all about pinpointing those self-defeating traits and changing them.

I have discovered that a certain group of psychological techniques coupled with a basic and universal law of nature called Reversion to the Mean can help people change attitudes and behaviors quickly and safely.

I will discuss this law of nature and explain in detail the psychological techniques that I recommend. They are simple and effective. You will not be playing games with your head when you use them. You will still be the person you always were— only better and happier. You will have made the best of your worst and given yourself a second chance for love, happiness and success.

*Chapter Two*

# WHAT YOU NEED TO KNOW ABOUT CHANGE

## What You Can Change and What You Can't and Why Women Handle Change Better

AN IMPORTANT FACT you should know about change is that women tend to handle it far better than men. Men really detest change. It is the rare man who, even under doctor's orders, will change from a couch potato to a bicyclist, or substitute halibut for hamburger.

The changes that men accept happily have to do with progress toward success. A man is as happy as a clam when he gets a promotion, a significant step up that involves a move from Grundy Center to the home office in Dallas. And he is tickled pink the day he trades in the old reliable Honda for a status-symbol Cadillac or Mercedes.

But move the living-room furniture around or tell the dear man you have signed the two of you up for a class in ballroom dancing, and one might think that you had suggested selling one of the children.

Tell a woman that you think the wing chair would look better in the other corner, or that her upper arms are getting flabby, or that her voice is too shrill—and she will snap into action. Before you know it, she'll be dragging the wing chair across the room, signing up for time in the weight room at the Y or making an appointment with a speech therapist.

A lot of this is nurture, not nature. Women take these kinds of changes in their stride because they have been made aware of their faults and deficiencies since childhood.

"Jenna is so gawky. Nothing looks right on her. . . ." "Karen is terribly stubborn. I tell her she has to learn to share. . . ." "Patricia has terrible hair. Absolutely no body and it's that awful mousy color. . . ." "Trudy is stubborn, just like my aunt. She's going to have a hard time in life if she doesn't change."

Girls grow up hearing about their behaviors and their appearances and the need to improve them discussed endlessly with family and friends. This conditions them to change. It also tends to give many women a very shaky self-image, and I have a lot to say about that later in this book.

Little boys, on the other hand, hear mostly good things about themselves. Even traits that might be considered faults are looked on with approval. "Jim is stubborn. Just like his father. . . ." "Saul is bossy. He'll be a big executive or maybe President when he grows up. . . ." "I never believed a child could be as strong-minded as our Bob." And so most boys grow up thinking they are fine fellows. What's to change? Ah, if they only knew!

Change is seductive and frightening, in equal proportions. I suspect that a solid majority of the population is attracted to the idea of change, since every year I meet thousands and thousands of people who tell me that they wish they could change their lives. Their marriages are less than perfect. Their sex lives are ho-hum. They are sad. They are bored. They are lonely, over-stressed, overweight. Their in-laws drive them crazy. Their boss is unreasonable.

It is not that they are singularly maladjusted and dissatisfied.

Not at all. By and large the people I meet as I travel around the country, giving lectures and seminars and as a corporate consultant, reflect a fairly typical economic and social cross-section of the population. No different from the math teacher who lives next door, or your boss's husband, or the Meals-on-Wheels driver who delivers a hot meal to your elderly father every day.

Nevertheless, they are convinced that other people are more in command of their lives, happier and more successful. It does not seem to occur to them that those others may feel equally inadequate. But they do.

Study after study has shown that deep down, most people are not satisfied with themselves or their lives. They yearn for a new start, a new life, a second chance. On the whole, this is a positive characteristic if it is not carried to an extreme. Our constant striving to better our lives has brought us from the cave to the skyscraper. But the changes many people envisage are unachievable. They dream a truly impossible dream of total makeover, a kind of rebirth.

Recently, I was shocked to attention on hearing a woman say, "I was dealt such a bum hand in life! I'm dealing myself a whole new hand." A talk show was on the television in my hotel room in Los Angeles, but I had not been paying much attention until I heard this. It was almost an exact echo of what an attractive and successful woman had told me a few hours earlier after a lecture I had given before a group of West Coast executives. "Life dealt me a rotten hand of cards," she had said, "and I'm ready to throw them all back and start off fresh with a new hand."

The coincidence startled me. So did the readiness of both women to throw in the cards life had dealt them and take their chances with a new hand. The woman I had met that afternoon obviously had some very good cards going for her. There was no guarantee that her new cards would be better.

It is seductive to dream of a total transformation, but we are what we are—the products of our genetic heritage. Both our basic physical characteristics and temperament are fixed before birth. Long-range studies of newborns show that infants described as easy or fussy, nervous or calm, happy or difficult, or tense or relaxed have the same temperament when they are adults. It may be more or less accentuated, but the style of their reaction to life is essentially unchanged. We cannot escape our inner person, the core that makes us what we are. Hollywood's finest may effect physical change with the aid of plastic surgery. But no matter how much they alter their appearance, they are still the same inside. And they always will be.

Most people are far better than they believe, and there is no reason for them to even consider a total transformation. Their discontent with themselves is usually provoked by a psychological "splinter." If you have a nasty, festering splinter in the sole of your foot, the pain and discomfort take precedence over everything else that is happening until the splinter is tweezed out and the infection treated.

In the same way, if one particular behavior or attitude of yours is self-defeating, it infects everything you do and think and feel. You want to get rid of the pain and start all over again from scratch, but a psychological splinter cannot be tweezed out. And need not be. And *should* not be.

All you really have to do is get rid of the infection caused by that splinter. And to do that, you must bring the disagreeable behavior or trait under control. Tune it up or tune it down, but don't throw it out. After modifying a trait, many people discover that what they considered a fault has become one of their greatest strengths.

The second chances that you have in life are not to start from scratch and create a new and perfect self, but to identify and modify whatever it is that is self-defeating and blocking you from getting what you want out of life. If you try to remake yourself into some ideal person, you will fail. You cannot escape that inner core.

But you *can* calibrate these innate characteristics, bringing them a few degrees closer to the norm. For instance, if you are a busybody, you can, for instance, fine-tune that aspect of your personality so that people will see you as a caring person who is interested in others rather than an officiously inquisitive pest.

Many self-defeating traits tend to be self-imposed obstacles—habits or characteristics that we have picked up along the road of life, usually without realizing it. While they may not be part of our inner core, the fact that we have adopted them means that at one time they had some value to us. They can often be modified so that they will be valuable again. Suppose that as a teenager you decided that the way to be popular was to always go along with what your friends said, and to keep your opinions to yourself. Unfortunately, as an adult, this attitude leads people to perceive you as a woman without a thought in her head. While it is true that no one likes a constantly carping critic, people respect a person who has ideas of her own and is not afraid to disagree when the occasion calls for it. Just a few degrees of change can turn this self-defeating behavior into an asset. And when you have brought it closer to the norm, you will not only feel liberated, you will discover that people like you better.

No matter how seductive change may be, it can also be frightening. Life dishes out change the way advertisers churn out junk mail. Like death and taxes, change is inevitable. There is no avoiding it—good or bad.

Too many people think of change as some great, overwhelming event, a tidal wave that will transform their lives in unexpected and unwanted ways. This kind of unavoidable change is frightening indeed. Wars, hurricanes, earthquakes, fires, disease and similar forces beyond our control have the power to change lives drastically.

But optional changes, the ones we choose to make ourselves as opposed to the ones that life dumps on us, should not be the least bit intimidating. They are comforting, because they feel right. We are correcting a fault and that makes us feel better about ourselves. And they are exhilarating, because we are getting that second chance in life that we want.

Change is growth, both intellectual and emotional. People who are open to change enjoy life far more than those who are bogged down in a static status quo. You can change your self-defeating traits yourself. You don't need a therapist or psychologist. You can control the process. And, because you are not under the intolerable strain of attempting the impossible, of trying to achieve a total makeover, your everyday life will remain on an even keel during the process.

Nor need you worry that you will go too far—that, for instance, you risk trading in your stinginess for extravagant generosity. This is impossible. First of all, as I said, we are what we are. We are always true to our inner core. And second, there is that wonderful law of nature, Reversion to the Mean, that governs the extent of any change we initiate ourselves. And I tell you all about it in the following chapter.

So if you decide that your life would be more rewarding if you were not going around with a chip on your shoulder all the time, or if you were able to make decisions without agonizing over them for days on end, then go ahead. Transform that psychological splinter that is infecting your life into a strength, and you will always be glad that you did.

# Chapter Three

# REVERSION TO THE MEAN

## The Natural Law That Protects You from Extremes

THE GOLDEN MEAN, the middle ground where the happy and healthy personality abides, is different for everyone. You should not try to tailor your characteristics and behavior to conform to some arbitrary norm. That way lies mediocrity.

Suppose, for instance, you are extravagantly generous. This is a wonderful trait. It is extreme but certainly not self-defeating—

*Unless* your generosity embarrasses its recipients.

*Unless* your generosity is an attempt to buy friendship or respect.

*Unless* your generosity leaves you without enough money to get through the rest of the month.

In such cases, your hypergenerosity is a self-defeating characteristic—

*Because* you are making others uncomfortable.

*Because* friendship and respect cannot be bought.

*Because* you are perpetually broke.

It would be wise to rein in your generosity, so that it will no longer act as a roadblock between you and friendship, respect and a balanced budget. And you need not worry that you will go to the other extreme. It is impossible to eradicate the generous component of your inner core, and there is also an invisible force, a natural phenomenon that will prevent you from turning into a tightfisted skinflint.

The law of nature known as Reversion to the Mean keeps you from going overboard when you are working to change a self-defeating trait. Generosity will never be transformed into stinginess. Shyness will never become brashness. If you are so pessimistic that you would never bet on the sun rising tomorrow, you will never believe that this is the best of all possible worlds. But you can adjust your gloomy outlook to the point where you are able to look forward to vacationing in Florida in February instead of being convinced that it will snow all the time you are there and that there will be alligators in the swimming pool.

Reversion to the Mean is a universal phenomenon. It applies to genetics as well as psychology, to the stock market as well as athletics, to examination grades as well as sexual mores. There is nothing magical or mysterious about it. It simply reflects the tendency of almost everything to seek the norm.

If you were to draw a picture of Reversion to the Mean, it would take the shape of what statisticians call a bell curve. Visualize it as two short lines separated by a dome. This curve illustrates all manner of quantities and qualities. Take trust, for instance.

If you are a very naive and trusting person, the kind who would buy the Brooklyn Bridge, you belong to the small group of people on the line at the left of the dome. There are no hard statistics available, but this probably encompasses some 5 to 10 percent of the population.

One film and television personality belongs here. A few years ago, he found himself millions in debt. His financial advisers, whom he had trusted, had wiped him out. "Almost overnight, everything I'd worked for was gone," he lamented.

Although he had been ill, arranging his affairs with so few controls shows this man to be an incredibly trusting soul.

Most of us are in the much, much larger group inside the dome. We trust people, but we are careful. We don't give our credit-card numbers out to strangers. We don't fall for "get-rich-quick" schemes, at least not very often. We lock the door when we leave the house. If our brother-in-law asks for a loan, we will probably give it to him, but if the teenager next door who has just totaled his heap wants to borrow our new car Saturday night, we will probably turn him down.

The line on the right of the dome encompasses the small group who find it very difficult to trust others. The farther they are to the right of the line, the less trusting they are. The range goes from those who check every price on their supermarket receipt and the addition on their restaurant checks to those who, even in times of national prosperity, bury cookie tins full of cash in the asparagus bed, because they are convinced that a catastrophe is in their future. As you reach the end of the line, the distrust verges on paranoia.

A significant proportion of the captains of industry are close to the end of this line. They do not trust anybody—except, just possibly, children under three. This total lack of trust, which could be seen as a fault on a personal level, is actually one of an entrepreneur's great assets, the secret of business success.

The New York builder Samuel LeFrak, for instance, lived by one rule all his business life—"Prepare for the worst and have a safety net ready"—and accumulated a two-billion-dollar empire in real estate, gas and oil fields and the entertainment world.

The same pattern exists in the way people see each other and the world around them. Perceptions of reality run the gamut from schizophrenia to depression. On the far left of the bell curve are people with schizophrenia, who have split off from reality and are delusional. The closer you get to the dome, the milder the distorted perception of reality becomes.

Most of us are in the dome itself. We have one characteristic in common—a mildly distorted vision of life. We tend to believe things are a little better than they really are. Studies have shown that the happiest couples see each other as better than they actually are. A certain degree of split from reality seems to make life more comfortable. On the other side of the dome, you have people with a strong grasp of reality. And most of them are depressed!

Studies involving two control groups—one depressed and one not—who were given tests to determine their perceptions of reality found that the depressed group was always the more accurate judge. Why should this be? Possibly because people who are depressed tend be more aware of the negative and see what is really there.

Reversion to the Mean does not apply only to such intangible attributes as trust and perception. It has universal applications. If it were not for this phenomenon, we would be living in a world of giants and pygmies, a world of extremely intelligent people and dullards. Geneticists have learned that height and intelligence, to use just two examples, show a strong drive to return to the norm.

A husband and wife who are both six feet tall might be expected to have a child who would eventually be six feet tall too. And some will. But more often, their child never grows to that height. The same thing holds true for a husband and wife who are brighter than average. Their child will probably be less intelligent than they are.

We are talking probabilities here. Some tall parents will have a tall child, and some genius parents may spawn another genius. But in the majority of cases, a child's height and intelligence will move toward the norm.

But what does all this mean to you and your desire to change for the better? How can this phenomenon help someone who is lonely or shy, a liar or a nag, or disappointed in the sexual side of her marriage?

It means that nature is on your side. You do not see it or feel it, but Reversion to the Mean acts like a magnet pulling you toward the golden mean, that middle ground between excess and deficit, where health and happiness reign. This does not mean that every behavior should be nudged into the area of the golden mean. Far from it. Who wants to be Jane Q. Average? Our singular mix of qualities—a few slightly exaggerated, a few somewhat weaker than the norm, and the majority somewhere in the middle—is what makes each one of us unique. What you want to do is moderate self-defeating behavior so that it is *somewhat* closer to the norm.

Let me give you a real-life example. When a top New York publishing executive heard I was writing this book, he confided that his worst fault had always been impulsiveness. He was always too quick to make decisions.

"As a result, I made more than my share of mistakes. When I realized that I was cutting my own throat, I surrounded myself with people who would slow me down, who would point out the pros and cons before I acted. I'm still fast off the mark, but these days I don't plunge ahead without considering the consequences."

In his case, he established a buffer zone—a staff that would ensure that he looked before he leaped. He had moved his behavior closer to the norm, not by changing himself and becoming less impulsive, but by changing his environment, surrounding himself with people who would force him to be more cautious. He was still impulsive, but now this trait worked *for* him, not against him.

Not all changes are as simple. Changes like the one the executive made, changes in environment, tend to be easier to make than changes from within. But not every impulsive soul is in a position to surround herself with a committee of naysayers to slow her down every time she is on the verge of succumbing to a $300 pair of shoes, or blowing her stack at her secretary or sales manager.

Fortunately, there are psychological techniques that are more effective because they produce change from within, change that is not dependent on outside monitors. I outline them for you in Part Two: Your Psychological Tool Kit. Together with the law of Reversion to the Mean, they will help you transform almost any undesirable trait into an asset.

*Part Two*

# ☑ YOUR PSYCHOLOGICAL TOOL KIT

## Professional Techniques for the Nonprofessional

Psychiatrists and psychologists routinely employ diagnostic and behavior-modification techniques to help patients. I see no reason why some of these professional "tools" should not be shared so that nonprofessionals can use them to tone down their self-defeating traits and behaviors themselves.

Over the years I have assembled a handful of psychological techniques that I have found to be especially useful and effective. They fall into three groups: List Techniques, Reinforcement Techniques and Rehearsal Techniques. I outline them in this section and illustrate their use. I also explain the workings of two psychological phenomena that accompany change: the Ripple Effect and the Halo Effect.

Together they make up a Psychological Tool Kit that you can refer back to and use for the rest of your life.

I also trace the experiences of four women who used a mixture of these techniques to modify their self-defeating traits so that they became strengths. They are:

Josie, whose abrasive manner and angry outbursts were endangering her position as the only female executive in a rust-belt manufacturing plant.

Rhonda, whose nagging was threatening her marriage.

Anabel, whose shyness had blocked her from making friends and moving ahead in her career.

Jessica, who was terrified of both change and decision-making to the extent that she risked losing a chance to fulfill her potential.

From their stories you will not only understand how each technique helped them, but you will learn how to choose and use the techniques that are right for you.

# Chapter Four

# THE LIST TECHNIQUES

## How to Pinpoint Self-Defeating Traits

BEFORE YOU CAN even try to change an undesirable trait, you have to zero in on exactly what it is that you need to change— and why. "But I know what my problem is," you say. Perhaps, and perhaps not.

On a subconscious level you may know yourself very well, but if you want to pinpoint the psychological splinter that is troubling you, you need to bring that knowledge up to the conscious level. Many a perfectionist, for instance, has incorrectly considered herself a run-of-the-mill procrastinator. Since different techniques are needed to modify each of these traits, a correct diagnosis is important.

Most people are convinced that they have a solid grasp of who and what they are—and yet, time after time, men and women who use my List Techniques tell me they are amazed at what they have learned about themselves. In many cases, they discover that traits they had considered faults were not faults at all. In fact, sometimes they did not have those traits at all!

The reason for this is that the way you see yourself is made up in large part of other people's perceptions—other people's often faulty perceptions. As a youngster, you may have been told that you were shy or thoughtless or selfish. After you have been told these "truths" about yourself over and over, they become internalized. Forever after, you believe you are selfish or thoughtless or shy, even though you may be just the opposite. Words can be as abusive as blows—and their effect can last a lifetime.

Even as adults, we tend to accept other people's assessments of ourselves. You are at a cocktail party and overhear Mrs. Armstrong say, "That woman is so *boring!*" while looking your way. Actually, she is talking about her next-door neighbor, but now and forever after, you wonder if people think you are boring. And your self-esteem drops into the cellar.

This is why I always recommend a kind of psychological surgery to cut away the false perceptions you have internalized over a lifetime and uncover the real you, with all your faults as well as your wonderful and endearing qualities. The psychological "scalpel" you use to cut away those false perceptions is the Basic Diagnostic List.

## THE BASIC DIAGNOSTIC LIST

This is unbiased, unemotional and absolutely discreet. Since no one but yourself will see this, you can be completely truthful in your assessment of your strengths and weaknesses. A serious self-diagnostic strategy, the Basic Diagnostic List yields a thumbnail psychological profile of the real you. Drawing up the list is simplicity in itself. All you need is pencil and paper.

Set aside a few minutes a week on the same day and at approximately the same time to make these lists. When you have finished, put each week's list away and do not look at them again until the fourth week.

You may discover that the qualities or their position on the list vary from week to week. You may also find that your goals change. This is to be expected as you gain insight into yourself.

### THE BASIC DIAGNOSTIC LIST

| Best Qualities | Worst Qualities | Goals |
|---|---|---|
| | FIRST WEEK | |
| 1. | 1. | 1. |
| 2. | 2. | 2. |
| 3. | 3. | 3. |
| | SECOND WEEK | |
| 1. | 1. | 1. |
| 2. | 2. | 2. |
| 3. | 3. | 3. |
| | THIRD WEEK | |
| 1. | 1. | 1. |
| 2. | 2. | 2. |
| 3. | 3. | 3. |

But do not worry if you feel no need to make changes. Some people are more aware of themselves.

The weekly intervals are important because during that time both your conscious and your subconscious will be at work. Do you really want to be a space pioneer? Are you really overbearing? Is honesty truly your best quality?

### FOURTH WEEK MASTER LIST

| | | |
|---|---|---|
| 1. | 1. | 1. |
| 2. | 2. | 2. |
| 3. | 3. | 3. |

On the fourth week, set aside time to work on your Master List. This is a synthesis of your three lists. If you changed them from week to week, it will require some analysis. Don't let this throw you. You do not need a degree in psychology, just plain common sense. Study your lists and write down your qualities in order of their strength and your goals in order of their importance. Give your third-week lists more weight than the others, since they are probably closer to the real you. When you are finished, study these qualities and goals. Are they compatible? Does one of your worst qualities block you from reaching your most important goal? Or one of your best qualities? A best quality can sometimes be self-defeating when considered in terms of a goal. For instance, if your goal is to win elective office and you consider that one of your best qualities is your willingness to speak your mind, this can be a roadblock. Politicians have to understand that at times silence is wisdom.

You should have no trouble in identifying self-defeating traits.

## Josie

Josie was a woman in a man's world, the production chief at a manufacturing plant outside Chicago, one of the few women and the only female executive in the company. The president and CEO was considering firing her because of her abrasive manner and nasty temper. "It's hard for the guys to handle it," he said, "since she's a woman. She's the source of a lot of bad feeling." But he was concerned about the flak he would get if he fired her. "She's the only woman exec, and production has gone up since she came here. I'll be a sitting duck for a discrimination suit."

"She sounds too good to fire," I said and asked if he would mind if I talked with her. "Once she faces the fact that her temper is cause for firing," I said, "she may see the light."

When I met with Josie, she insisted she was neither angry nor abrasive. "I just act that way because these guys are bone lazy."

"There may be better ways for you to motivate them," I said, "and you may be angrier than you realize." I told her a little about the Basic Diagnostic List, and she agreed to make one out.

Her Master List looked like this:

FOURTH WEEK MASTER LIST

| | | |
|---|---|---|
| 1. hot temper | 1. work hard | 1. marriage |
| 2. bossy | 2. efficient | 2. more money |
| 3. worrier | 3. plan ahead | 3. promotion |

When I met with her a month later, she reported she had been shocked to discover that her hair-trigger temper was her worst quality. Like most people who use the Diagnostic List, she had found herself thinking about her lists every day—searching for accuracy, thinking hard about her goals, weighing her best and worst qualities. She had come to realize how furiously and frequently she lost her temper.

"Your best qualities are fine assets for an executive," I pointed out. "They should help you get the promotion you want. And the money, too.

"Let's look at the qualities you consider your worst. How bad are they?

"Worrying is just another aspect of planning. And you consider your ability to plan ahead one of your best qualities. Worrying is foreseeing possible problems and thinking of ways to cope with or prevent them. It is a valuable trait if you don't carry it to extremes.

"In terms of your job—or of any human relationship—your quick temper and bossiness are definitely self-defeating. However, if you can rein them, they have positive aspects. Take bossiness. You cannot be an effective executive without being able to direct people, to deal with them in a fair and consistent manner and get the desired results. This is an asset. But if bossiness means being officious and brusque and using anger as a spur the way you do, that is self-defeating.

"Your hot temper heads your list of worst qualities. And you are right, it is the real problem. You are risking your future with your angry outbursts. Your colleagues resent them. Since you are a woman, they feel that they can't tell you to 'go to hell' or 'stuff it' or whatever they might tell each other. The men you supervise resent them even more. And your CEO is ready to fire you unless you can control your temper.

"An occasional and well-controlled show of anger can be extremely effective, a true management asset. But you have to choose your time and place carefully, and know what you want to accomplish," I told her. "If you want to stay with this company, you will have to control your temper instead of letting it control you.

"Now, your most important goal is marriage. Do you realize that you did not list a single quality that is conducive to an intimate relationship? Hard-working and efficient are fine qualities for a wife, but not enough. Few men want a wife who is bossy and hot-tempered and a worrywart. You don't seem to value qualities like warmth and understanding and humor. They are as important to your career as they are to an intimate relationship."

She sighed. "I have a lot to think about," she said, "but you've convinced me of one thing. I have to control my temper. I really want to stay with this company."

I will tell you how Josie worked to control her angry outbursts in the next chapter.

## THE CONDENSED DIAGNOSTIC LIST

This is not a timesaving substitute for the Basic Diagnostic List. It is designed as a personality-evaluation tool to be used when you are faced with a major decision. Don't bother with it if you are simply trying to make up your mind which brand of running shoes or microwave to buy. But with truly big decisions, ones that have the potential to change your life, like marriage, divorce, conception, a career shift or moving from one part of the country to another, the Condensed Diagnostic List is invaluable. It helps you determine whether or not the prospective change is compatible with who you are and what you want in life.

The Condensed Diagnostic List takes four days and demands intensive introspection. It is part of a two-step decision-making process.

FIRST, SECOND AND THIRD DAYS

| Best Qualities | Worst Qualities | Goals |
|---|---|---|
| 1. | 1. | 1. |
| 2. | 2. | 2. |
| 3. | 3. | 3. |
| 4. | 4. | |
| 5. | 5. | |
| 6. | 6. | |

Set aside a block of time for the first three days, and a bigger block on the fourth. Each day make a list of your six best and worst qualities in order of their strength and your three most desired goals in order of their importance. It takes time and thought to come up with six best and worst qualities, but keep at it until you are satisfied with each day's list. The qualities and goals and their orders will most likely change from day to day as you concentrate on who you are and what you want.

FOURTH DAY MASTER LIST

| | | |
|---|---|---|
| 1. | 1. | 1. |
| 2. | 2. | |
| 3. | 3. | |

On the fourth day, narrow the lists down to your three best and worst qualities and to your single most important goal.

Think about your qualities and how they may affect your ability to reach that goal. You may find that you are now clear about what you should do, but I suggest putting off your decision until you have completed the next step, your Worst-Case Scenario.

## THE WORST-CASE SCENARIO

When you face an important decision about a major change, use this technique after you have completed a Condensed Diagnostic List. You may want to make the change but are frightened of the possible consequences. Conversely, you may be reluctant to make the change, but worry that it might be a mistake not to. The Worst-Case Scenario will give you the perspective you need.

I also suggest that you use it after you have completed a Basic Diagnostic List and identified the self-defeating trait you want to modify. The Worst-Case Scenario will make it very clear why you need to modify that trait. You will be able to assess the difference it will make in your life if you modify that trait, and the results if you don't.

The Worst-Case Scenario involves making two lists:

1. The worst possible consequences of making the change you are considering.
2. The worst possible consequences of *not* making it.

Write down as many consequences as you can imagine. Think of the very worst that could happen. If time permits, put your two scenarios away for a few days. The more time your subconscious has to process them, the easier your choice will be. Even overnight is better than nothing.

Then study the two scenarios. Reread them carefully and analyze each drawback. Consider each consequence in terms of your Master List. Then ask yourself these two questions about each consequence:

1. How likely is it to happen?
2. What would I do if it did happen?

If you know what you would do if you made the change and the worst were to happen, you are probably ready to take the leap. After all, there are no sure things in life. Once you reach this point, ask yourself one more question:

Which will be better for me in the long run?

Your decision should be much clearer.

## Jessica

Although women adjust to change more readily than men, a woman who will whip off to the hairdresser as a redhead and emerge as a blonde without a dither can be dismayed at the prospect of moving away from her family in an upward career shift, a change that a man usually takes in stride. Leaving home and friends is much more of a wrench for a woman.

Jessica had been offered a promotion that involved a transfer from Atlanta to Los Angeles. The thought of moving 3,000 miles away from family and friends was daunting. "I'm going to turn it down," she told her brother-in-law after considering the offer. "My roots are here."

"What are you? A plant?" he asked. "Those aren't reasons. Those are excuses. Think it over again before you give them your decision."

She used the Condensed Diagnostic List. By the fourth night,

when she completed her Master List, she had done a lot of thinking about herself. Her Master List looked like this:

| Best | Worst | Goals |
|------|-------|-------|
| Loyal | Critical | Happiness |
| Honest | Set in my ways | |
| Stable | Fearful | |

She shook her head. This did not seem useful at first. Happiness was a terribly amorphous goal. And there did not seem
to be much difference between "stable" and "set in my ways,"
although she had listed one as a best and the other as
a worst quality. Both indicated a resistance to change. And so
did "fearful." Did this confirm her decision to turn down the
offer?

She decided to see what a Worst-Case Scenario would show.
It read this way:

*If I Turn Down the Promotion*
1. My boss will never feel the same about me again.
2. I'll probably never be offered another promotion.
3. I may end up looking for another job in a year or two.
4. I will always know that I had a chance at a great job, where
   I could prove myself, and I chickened out because I didn't
   want to leave home.

*If I Accept the Promotion*
1. I will be under a lot of stress for the first months.
2. I will be lonely. I will miss my friends and family desperately.
3. I may not be able to handle the job, and I'll be fired and
   stranded thousands of miles away from home.
4. I may hate the job and not get along with my coworkers,
   and resign. Then I'll be stranded, etc.
5. There might be an earthquake.

The longer she studied the two scenarios, the sillier her fears seemed. She would be too busy to be lonely at the beginning. She was sure to make friends at work. As for family—well, the fact was that she did not see them all that often. She could stay in touch with them by phone and see them on vacations, and her mother would be delighted to visit her.

Her boss would not have offered her the promotion if he did not think she could handle it, but if it did not work out, she would not be stranded. She had money in the bank, and she would be getting a significant salary increase.

As for an earthquake—well, if she stayed in Atlanta, there might be a hurricane.

She was surprised to discover how important that promotion had suddenly become to her. The more she thought about turning it down, the more she wanted it—even if it might be a bit of a gamble.

She had learned a lot about herself from these two List Techniques. She had learned that it was fear of change that was making her hesitant. She had realized that no matter whether she stayed in Atlanta or went to Los Angeles, her life would change. Change was inevitable.

And, most important, she came to understand that she had only one decision to make. Which way did she want her life to change? Did she want to take this opportunity, or did she want to wait passively for what the future might offer?

The next morning she told her boss that she was flattered by his faith in her and was looking forward to the challenges of the Los Angeles position.

*Chapter Five*

# OPERANT CONDITIONING

Positive and Negative Behavior-Changers

OPERANT CONDITIONING CONSISTS of three types of Reinforcement—Positive, Intermittent and Negative—all of them designed to change behavior. Positive and Negative Reinforcement will help you modify your own behavior. All three can help you modify someone else's behavior, although Negative Reinforcement should be used in very small doses, or it becomes self-defeating.

Before I tell you how to use these techniques, let me tell you how rats react to Operant Conditioning. Students of clinical psychology have done experiments with rats that teach as much about people as they do about rats. One of the classics is a three-part experiment based on the findings of Dr. B. F. Skinner, the father of Operant Conditioning.

The experiment has three parts. In the first, a rat is put into a cage that is empty except for a metal bar on one side. The first thing the rat does is explore the cage. The hungrier it is, the more exploring it does. It sniffs at the corners of the cage and stretches up against its walls.

Eventually the rat bumps into the metal bar. When it does, a food pellet is released. This causes the rat to step up its explorations around the area where the food appeared. Sooner or later, it hits the bar again and gets another pellet. The rat soon learns that pushing the bar produces food. Now, when it is hungry, it pushes the bar.

This is learned behavior. Left to themselves, rats do not go around pressing bars. The pressing response was learned because it produced food. The food is a *Positive Reinforcement,* a reward.

In the second part of the experiment, the metal bar is programed differently. Sometimes the rat gets a food pellet—and sometimes zilch. It continues to press the bar even though most of the time nothing happens. It is almost as if the rat had said to itself, "I'll just keep on pressing that bar and see what happens." This is *Intermittent Reinforcement.* It does not alter the rat's behavior. The rat is rewarded just often enough to make it worth its while to continue pressing the bar.

The success of slot machines in gambling casinos is due to Intermittent Reinforcement. People sit in front of them hour after hour, feeding quarter after quarter into them even though they rarely hit a jackpot, because they know that sometimes they do pay off.

The third part of the experiment is somewhat more complicated. It involves two rats, Julie and Debbie, in separate cages, who have learned to press the bar to get food. Julie presses the bar in her cage and gets a slight electric shock. This is *Negative Reinforcement.* She stops pressing the bar. Debbie presses the bar in her cage and gets nothing at all—no shock, no food. She keeps on pressing, but she never gets anything. As time goes by, Debbie presses the bar less and less often and finally she stops altogether.

However, if you wait long enough, you will see Julie, who received the Negative Reinforcement, go up to the bar and press it again. If she does not get a shock, she will keep on pressing it time after time, even though she gets no food. Before she gives up, she will have pressed the bar approximately the same number of times as Debbie.

What does all this add up to? It shows that while a punishment or Negative Reinforcement will suppress a behavior for a while, it does not change the behavior or get rid of it. Despite the shocks Julie experienced, they were not enough to change her behavior permanently. The most effective way to change a behavior whether in rats or yourself or your significant other is to provide Positive Reinforcement.

## POSITIVE REINFORCEMENT

This is the single most powerful psychological tool for producing change. And a very pleasant one to use. It is the equivalent of a pat on the back, although sometimes it can feel like winning the lottery.

### How to Influence Someone Else's Behavior

Positive Reinforcement is all about rewards. It is based on encouraging desired behavior. A nod, a smile, a kiss or a hug, a word of praise—all do wonders in encouraging a behavior in someone else.

I used Positive Reinforcement to get my husband to make the breakfast coffee every morning. It was nothing I had planned; it simply happened. Milt never lifted a finger around the house except to turn on the television when there was a football game. His mother had always waited on him hand and foot, as I did after we were married, and he thought this was the way things should be. When, after decades of marriage, an opportunity to encourage him to perform a minor chore—making the breakfast coffee—presented itself, I took advantage of it.

I had bought a new coffeemaker, the kind that not only brews coffee, but grinds the beans as well. Milt was a sucker for gadgets and he had to try it out the minute I unwrapped it. The next day he came home with half a dozen kinds of coffee beans. Every morning he put a different combination of beans through the grinder and brewed the coffee until he came up with a blend that we both agreed was great.

I remember that morning well. I praised his coffee to the skies, showered him with compliments about the way he had experimented with the different varieties of coffee beans until he came up with the perfect brew.

I knew Milt would eventually get bored with his new toy unless I gave him a lot of encouragement, a lot of Positive Reinforcement. He started making our morning coffee because he wanted to play with this new gadget, but he continued to make it because I praised him so much during his experiments.

I would taste the coffee every morning and tell him very seriously just what I thought about the flavor and aroma. He liked the attention. The morning he hit on the blend we finally settled on and that I still drink, I told him he had attained perfection. And I kept on telling him that morning after morning.

## How to Modify Your Own Behavior

When it comes to rewarding yourself as you nudge your self-defeating trait closer and closer toward the norm, the sky is the limit. I am serious about this. Rewards are very important. When you try to change a behavior, you are taking something away from yourself. Granted that you will be better off without it, nonetheless, you will feel a loss. It is important to replace that negative with a positive, to give yourself a pat on the back every time you make it through the day without nagging, swearing, yelling at the kids or dithering over minor decisions. Paste a gold star on the calendar, call a friend long distance, or put a couple of dollars aside toward a more substantial pat on the back, like an evening at the theater, a pair of high-heeled red sandals or the piano lessons you have always wanted to take. Squirrel away your Positive Reinforcement dollars and you will soon have enough to indulge yourself. The bonus here is that if you really want those red sandals, you will curb that self-defeating trait even sooner.

There are all kinds of Positive Reinforcements. Every once in a while, I make the mistake of taking on too many commitments, and I find myself rushing around trying to prepare a lecture, do research for a seminar, write my column and make notes for my television spot. The term "rushing around like a chicken with her head cut off" is a pretty good description of me at these times.

When I realize what a tizzy I'm in, I drop everything and write the words "I have everything under control" on several three-by-five index cards. I tape one on the bathroom mirror, another on my dressing table mirror, one on the refrigerator, another on the cupboard over the sink and another next to my office telephone. It works. Just writing the message begins to calm me down, and each time I see one of those index cards, I'm reassured that I will fulfill each of my commitments. And I always do.

Other people have used messages like "I am always prompt" or "I never yell at the kids" or "I never talk more than five minutes on the telephone" or "I am always on time for my appointments." Once you start thinking about how to give yourself Positive Reinforcement, you will come up with a dozen ways to give yourself that encouraging pat on the back.

On those days that your self-defeating trait gets the better of you—and there will be such days—do not let yourself be discouraged. I repeat this. *Do Not Let Yourself Be Discouraged.* That leads to failure. On days like this, you need even more Positive Reinforcement. Tell yourself, "I'm going to do better tomorrow. I don't like this kind of behavior and I'm going to rein it in. I know I can do it."

### Serendipitous Reinforcement

This is a particularly wonderful kind of Positive Reinforcement, because it is completely unexpected. It may spring from something someone did or said. A television producer I work with occasionally told me that something I had said a few years before had changed her life. "It did?" I could not remember any momentous life-changing statement I had made.

"I was telling you about an award I had been given. And how I felt that I really did not deserve it, that it should have gone to someone with more experience and more credits. And you said—*Of course you deserve it. You're a woman of status!*

"Ever since then, whenever I get to feeling inadequate, and that's at least once a week, I tell myself—*You're a woman of status.* And I immediately regain faith in myself."

Few people recognize the power that lies in a compliment or a criticism. Both have a strong effect on a person's self-image—one for the better, the other for the worse. So think twice before making negative comments—and be generous with your favorable ones.

Other Serendipitous Reinforcements are a by-product of your efforts to curb a self-defeating trait, something you did yourself that was a breakthrough of one kind or another.

## Josie

One of the problems Josie faced in trying to control her temper was that the men she supervised resented not only having a woman boss, but being the defenseless targets of her angry outbursts as well. As a result their performance was often below par, which provoked more angry tirades.

"One day when I just couldn't keep myself from popping off to the foreman about the way a piece of machinery had been maintained," Josie told me, "I took a deep breath—and smiled."

"And that worked?" I asked. "You were able to control your temper?"

"Well, it seemed to take the edge off things. I was able to tell the foreman 'This is a hell of a way to treat machinery. Didn't your mother teach you to take care of your toys?'

"I couldn't believe that I said it. It was so ridiculous I had to laugh. And so did he. He put a crew on it right off and I haven't had to ride herd on that particular problem since."

Josie had discovered the power of laughter and smiles. They tend to disarm others and make them more agreeable, more disposed to cooperate. The physical and the psychological are closely linked. When you smile or laugh, you feel better because the muscles involved compress the blood vessels in your face. The pressure forces blood up to your brain, and the surge of blood causes the brain to order an increase in the production of endorphins, substances that make you feel better and more relaxed. One smile usually provokes another, so you have two people whose brains are ordering up extra endorphins and they both feel a little better, a little more at one with the world and each other.

In Josie's case, the silly bit of humor and the laughter had a two-pronged effect. First of all, it disarmed the foreman and produced the result she wanted. Instead of having to defend himself against criticism, he could share in the humor of her remark. If she had blown her top, which would have been Negative Reinforcement, he would undoubtedly have been sullen and taken his time about getting that piece of machinery working properly again. This way, he put someone on the job immediately. She had substituted humor and laughter for an angry blast—and got an instant result.

And second, this instant success with the foreman made her feel great. It was a moment she could remember with pleasure. And this breakthrough had given her a new psychological tool for dealing with people—humor.

Serendipitous Reinforcements should be stored away in your mental bank and drawn out from time to time as you need them.

## INTERMITTENT REINFORCEMENT

This now-and-then encouragement technique is used on other people. It is a vital next step after Positive Reinforcement when you are trying to modify someone else's behavior. Once a desired behavior has become partially established in another person, you should cut down on Positive Reinforcement and substitute Intermittent Reinforcement, which is always positive, but less frequent.

If you want to encourage your husband to empty the dishwasher, for instance, give him lots of Positive Reinforcement the first five or six days, but then bite your tongue. Don't say anything the next two times he empties it. You might give him a big hug the third time and tell him how helpful he is. Again, don't say anything the next three times. Then tell him how much you love him and appreciate his taking over this chore. Little by little, make the intervals between Positive Reinforcements longer and longer, but never cut them out entirely.

The reason for cutting down on a steady dose of Positive Reinforcement is that after a while, praise and approval lose their power to affect behavior. They become taken for granted. They are just words, the equivalent of the meaningless "Have a good day" or "We must get together soon."

Intermittent Reinforcement is infrequent and unexpected, and thus carries a stronger message. And the message should be worded differently each time. Don't let it become automatic. When you tell your husband what a great help it is when he empties the dishwasher, make it count. Let him know that he is a prince among men.

I did exactly this with my husband so that he would continue making coffee in the morning. After a while I switched to Intermittent Reinforcement. Instead of every morning, I told Milt twice a week how good his coffee was. Then once a week. And then just every now and then. I made sure my compliments meant something. One morning, for instance, I told him that if he ever left me for a younger woman, I planned to drop in on them every morning for coffee, because no one made coffee as good as his. He liked that.

Now, I would never compare my husband to a rat, but his behavior paralleled that of the rats in that three-part experiment. Intermittent Reinforcement provided just enough of a reward to keep him interested. He never felt that I took his coffee-making for granted, and I rationed my praise so that he would not take that for granted either.

## NEGATIVE REINFORCEMENT

Positive Reinforcement encourages a behavior. Negative Reinforcement discourages a behavior. Positive Reinforcement is hugging your husband when he does the laundry. Negative Reinforcement is telling him he used too much detergent.

Negative Reinforcement is a short-term technique and is most effective when used to curb your own self-defeating trait. It should be immediate and usually physical. Every occurrence of the undesired behavior should be discouraged instantly. A physical discouragement is usually the easiest to administer on the spot. (Parents should not take this as an endorsement of spanking. It is not.)

There are many ways to provide this kind of Negative Reinforcement. Some people make themselves run up and down stairs every time they exhibit the undesired behavior. Some scrub the bathroom or wax the kitchen floor or wash a window. Others jump rope for five minutes or do twenty sit-ups. The important thing is that the "punishment" be immediate. Depriving yourself of a predinner cocktail or of watching a favorite television program are not effective forms of Negative Reinforcement. You may forget that you were not going to have a drink or you may tell yourself, "I know I should not have nagged Jim about getting the car inspected, and I won't do it again. So there's no reason I can't watch the show."

Negative Reinforcement is seldom effective in modifying someone else's behavior as the experiment with the rats made clear. If it were, the naggers of this world would be sitting in the catbird seat. I know. I used to nag my husband.

Milt smoked like a furnace and I was always after him to stop. It was not that he was unaware of the risks. After all, he was a physician. But even after he developed hypertension and his own doctor warned him to stop, he kept right on. Nothing I said had any effect.

Then he developed a heart flutter and his doctor put him on medication. Milt told me this was it. He was going to quit. And he did, for a couple of weeks. A year later he developed bladder cancer, the fifth most common cancer in men. Approximately half the men who die from it are heavy smokers. Milt was one of them.

My nagging had accomplished absolutely nothing at all, except to annoy my husband. You cannot make someone do something he does not want to do. As a psychologist, I knew this, but as a wife, I did not. Looking back, I am full of regret that I allowed a self-defeating trait like nagging to shadow so many hours of our life together.

So when a young friend of my daughter told me that her marriage was on the verge of collapse because of her nagging, I had to do my best to help her.

## Rhonda

A working wife with an eight-month-old baby, Rhonda was constantly nagging her husband to help her around the house. "I know I shouldn't, but I just can't help myself," she said. "I drop the baby off at day care in the morning, spend eight hours in the office and pick the baby up on my way home. When I get there, Bob's reading the paper. I feed Lucy and bathe her and play with her a little before I put her to bed. Then I still have to get supper. I'm always tired and angry. He doesn't do a thing, even when I ask him.

"Last night I asked him to take the garbage out at least three times. When he finally took it out, he slammed the door so hard that he broke the window. If it weren't for the baby, I think I'd leave him."

*   *   *

Women have always nagged because their husbands never want to visit her folks or wait too long between haircuts or refuse to go shopping with her, but these are peripheral and minor nags. The nitty-gritty nagging about who does what around the house is the serious stuff. And it is increasing these days with the proliferation of dual-career marriages.

When it comes to running the house, women almost automatically take command, and many husbands feel put upon when asked to help with domestic chores, which rank at the very bottom of the pleasure scale. When 800 married men were asked how they felt about helping with housework, most said they resented being told what to do and usually ignored their wives' requests. "Men are inclined to resist even the slightest hint that anyone, especially a woman, is telling them what to do," confirms Professor Deborah Tannen of Georgetown University.

When Rhonda asked Bob to take out the garbage, his reaction had been to wait a while before complying with her request, which he experienced as an order. By taking his own sweet time, he would not feel he was being bossed around. When Rhonda asked a second time, he put it off again. And when she asked the third time . . . !

"You have to eliminate the resentment factor," I told Rhonda, "and make him feel good about helping around the house."

She rolled her eyes.

"It can be done," I assured her. "But only if you stop nagging. Right now. Nagging is Negative Reinforcement and self-defeating. The more you nag, the more he will resist. I suggest you use Negative Reinforcement on yourself instead."

I recommended a rather forceful version. "Get a strong rubber band that fits loosely on your wrist so it won't cut off your circulation, and wear it every day. Whenever you catch yourself nagging, just snap that band. Hard, so that it really stings. If you do this every time you start to nag, I promise you will cut down on your nagging.

"And every night, give yourself Positive Reinforcement. Tell yourself—'I nagged Bob about the way he always leaves his dirty underwear on the floor and about forgetting to pick up Lucy's vitamin drops today, but that was all. Just two nags. I'm doing better.' Or 'I really deserve a pat on the back. This makes the third day without nagging.'"

This double-barreled technique of Negative and Positive Reinforcement gets almost immediate results. I told Rhonda she would probably notice a significant reduction in her nagging within three or four days.

I also advised her to stop asking Bob to do anything around the house. "If he does something on his own initiative, fine. If he doesn't, just live with it. Before you can get him to help, you have to get rid of the emotional tension that has built up between the two of you."

"Great!" Rhonda was bitter. "I just smile and do all the work."

"Your time will come," I promised her. "Right now you are setting the stage for the next act."

With the aid of her rubber-band bracelet, Rhonda's nagging was almost nonexistent after three weeks. She no longer got upset when Bob did not do what she asked, because she was not asking him to do anything. And Bob no longer had anything to resent. Peace and harmony had been restored. The stage was set for a breakthrough.

It came the night she had to work late. She called Bob and asked if he would pick the baby up from the day-care center, just this once. When she got home Bob and the baby were in the kitchen. Lucy was in her high chair, her face smeared with apple sauce. Bob was singing old Cole Porter songs to amuse her. And Rhonda joined in.

Finally she said, "You must be starving. What do you want to do? Put her to bed? Or start supper?"

"You get supper," he said. "I'll put her to bed."

What was left of the evening was happy and relaxed. Rhonda did a lot of exclaiming about how helpful he had been and how good he was with the baby. "It's a long time since we've had such fun," she said as they were getting ready for bed. "I really appreciate your picking Lucy up."

"No big deal," he said. "It was sort of interesting, all those little kids. There were a couple of other fathers there. I said I'd probably be seeing them again." And then he suggested, "Why don't I take over the day-care run? It's on my way from work. That way you would have a little more time at each end of the day."

Rhonda couldn't believe it. He offered! Out of a clear blue sky!

She had made two very intelligent moves that evening. First, she did not tell Bob to either put the baby to bed or start supper. She *asked* him which he would rather do. He had no sense of being ordered around. She had also given him generous amounts of Positive Reinforcement during the evening.

For his part, Bob had been surprised to see other fathers picking up their children, something he had always considered an exclusively feminine responsibility. And Rhonda's sincere appreciation for his helping her in the emergency had made him feel pretty special.

The stage was set for a grand gesture. He made it because he thought he would enjoy it. But he also understood for the first time how rushed and harried Rhonda was in the evenings. Not that she had not told him so a hundred times. But that night he was ready to accept the fact without having to be told.

This could never have been planned. But if it had not been this particular set of circumstances, it would have been another that would have provided a breakthrough. As I told Rhonda, once the stage is set, action is certain to follow.

Rhonda still nags every now and then. But not enough to disrupt their relationship. Because it is infrequent, Bob now takes it as an expression of loving concern for him and their daughter and their home. Bit by bit, he has taken over a few more chores. And Rhonda has lowered her housekeeping standards. "After all," she told me, "love is more important than the garbage."

## THE REINFORCEMENT LIST

The final Operant Conditioning technique is the Reinforcement List. This pinpoints the whens, whys and effects of your self-defeating trait, and helps your brain help you. You will need a little notebook for your list that you can tuck into your handbag or your pocket, so that it will always be handy.

This psychological tool consists of:

1. A daily list of every time the trait or attitude you are trying to modify crops up. Write down the time and the circumstances in your notebook. The entries should be brief. Don't go into a lot of detail.
2. An end-of-the-day evaluation, which consists of writing answers to the following questions. If a question is not pertinent, ignore it. The last one, for instance, may not apply to every situation.

   A. Did I gain anything when I did this? If so, what?
   B. Did I lose anything when I did this? If so, what?
   C. Was there another way I could have handled the situation? If so, how?
   D. How did it make me feel?
   E. How do I think it made the other person feel?

3. A weekly evaluation of your progress to see what patterns emerge and what progress you have made.

## Josie

Josie used the Reinforcement List to help subdue the hot temper that was sabotaging her relationships with her colleagues and the men she supervised. Here are one day's entries and evaluations:

OCCURRENCES

*9:45—I popped off at Ed because the time sheets weren't on my desk.*

*11:00—Blew my top when I discovered the guys smoking on the line. They know it is against the fire regulations. I really tore into them.*

*3:30—Blasted the electrician. He cut off the power for half an hour to make a repair. Told him he should have done it on the weekend.*

EVALUATIONS

1. *I probably overreacted. Ed is usually very reliable. It might have been better just to ask why he hadn't turned them in on time.*

2. *I could have handled this better. Perhaps I should have posted a memo on the bulletin board. Or asked the foreman to take care of it. The crew was pretty sullen the rest of the day. We didn't reach the target quota, because some of their production was rejected as below standard.*

3. *I should have kept my mouth shut. He was just doing his job. I hope I don't have to ask him to do anything in the near future. He was ready to wring my neck.*

If you are conscientious about making your daily entries and evaluations, you will almost certainly have made progress on whatever behavior you want to amend by the time your first weekly evaluation rolls around. One woman told me, "It seems magical the way I've been able to cut down on my bossy mother-knows-best attitude in such a short time."

There is no magic involved. What you do have going for you is something better—your brain, that often underutilized organ. Studies have shown that writing down each occurrence of an unwanted behavior tends to reduce the number of occurrences. This is because there is a direct link between one's perceptions and one's behavior. Once the brain incorporates the message that a certain behavior is not productive or desirable, it goes to work to extinguish or reduce that behavior. The more ways your brain perceives something, the faster the behavior will be minimized.

Here are three additional ways to implement the effectiveness of the Reinforcement List:

1. Each night after you have written your evaluations, read them aloud.
2. Give yourself a dose of Positive Reinforcement every night before you go to bed. Tell yourself, "I've made real progress in the last two days" or "I know I'm going to reach my goal"—whatever seems right to you as long as it is positive and encouraging.
3. Stand in front of a mirror and look yourself straight in the eye when you administer that dose of Positive Reinforcement.

One reason for reviewing your lists every week is to spot patterns. When Josie reviewed her entries at the one-week mark, she found a definite pattern. She tended to lose her temper before thinking about the best way to handle any given incident. She realized that if she had given herself a minute to consider the whys and wherefores of each situation, she could have handled them more effectively. She also realized that she lost more than she gained by her temper outbursts. This kind of result-oriented, bottom-line reasoning strengthened her determination to control her temper.

No matter what self-defeating trait you are trying to tone down, you will find a pattern in your Reinforcement List. You may find that it gets the better of you at certain times of day. Late in the afternoon perhaps, when you are tired. Or when you are nervous or coping with stress. There may be more incidents on certain days—Fridays or weekends.

Once you see a pattern in your behavior, try to alter that pattern. Unless, of course, it is a pattern of diminishing occurrences. In that case, don't change a thing.

But suppose that, like Josie, your self-defeating trait is a temper that flashes out of control, and you discover that you lose your temper more often when you have been up late the night before. It would be wise to confine your late nights to weekends. And if you tend to lose your temper in the late afternoon, take a coffee break in the middle of the afternoon or go for a walk. If you are at home or fortunate enough to have a private office, give yourself ten minutes alone with the door closed. Just sit back and relax. Close your eyes and pay attention to your breathing. I find this kind of ten-minute escape extremely helpful when I am under a lot of pressure. I have a little mantra that I use when I feel overstressed. I breathe in, thinking "everything" and I breathe out, thinking "is possible." Ten minutes of this and I'm completely relaxed and ready for anything.

Since it takes approximately six weeks to three months to establish a new behavior, I suggest you maintain your Reinforcement List for at least two months. If the unwanted behavior crops up again later, get out your notebook and work on your Reinforcement List for another month.

Remember, you are not trying to stamp out that trait or behavior, just to rein it in so that it is no longer a roadblock preventing you from happiness and success.

# Chapter Six

# THE REHEARSAL TECHNIQUES

## How to Turn Wishes into Reality

THIS THIRD GROUP of psychological tools, the Rehearsal Techniques—Acting As If and Previsualization—are a bit like the fairy godmother's magic wand. They can transform you into the person you should be and can be. With them, you get to be your own fairy godmother. You write your own script, cast yourself as the star of your own drama and rehearse your role until it is no longer a role but reality.

### ACTING AS IF

The name explains the technique, a form of psychological role-playing. If you are frightened, Act As If you were courageous. If you believe you are unattractive, Act As If you were a beauty. If you are cold and aloof, Act As If you were friendly and outgoing. The world will perceive you as assured and attractive and friendly. And eventually you will be more courageous, feel more attractive and be more outgoing.

But you will still be you. The inner core that makes you special will not change. Nor should it. If you are an introvert and you feel that is self-defeating, it is important to understand that you will never become an extrovert. Nor should you want to. All you want to do is become less introverted—to reduce your aloofness and strengthen your more sociable qualities. You simply want to tweak your behavior closer to the norm so that your introversion will no longer be a barrier between you and the rest of the world.

## Anabel

Twenty-nine-year-old Anabel thought she was beyond hope. She was so shy that if she could have crawled under a rock, she would have. Slim and tall, she would have been attractive if she had not hunched her shoulders and ducked her head so that she did not look people in the eye. She thought of herself as a gawky scarecrow. And so did other people, because that was the image she projected.

She was lonely, she told me, because she was too shy to make friends. She did not know how to talk to people. She was worried that her advertising agency job was going nowhere because she was too shy to push her ideas when dealing with clients. "And I hate my looks," she said fiercely.

Shyness may be rather sweet in a five-year-old, but it can be a devastatingly self-defeating trait in an adult. It restricts your life in almost every way. Shyness makes you focus inward on yourself instead of outward on the world and all it has to offer. As a result, the shy person never develops her full potential, because she is locked into her own emotional jail.

Almost everyone suffers fleeting attacks of shyness, but a surprisingly large percentage of the population is self-defeatingly, day-in-day-out shy. If, like Anabel, you belong to this group, the key to your emotional jail is now in your possession. You can use the Rehearsal Technique of Acting As If to unlock the cell door and put an end to your solitary confinement.

\* \* \*

I explained this to Anabel and added, "As for your looks, you can look better in seconds. Just stand up straight." From the look she gave me, I could tell she thought my advice was the equivalent of "take two aspirins and call me in the morning."

"I'm serious." I led her to a full-length mirror. "Stand tall. Shoulders back. Head high. Face the world." I felt like a drill sergeant. "There! That is the real Anabel. You look one hundred percent better.

"This is more than a matter of correcting your posture. This is Acting As If. From now on, try to stand tall and walk tall. It makes you look more attractive and self-assured. Try to Act As If you were full of self-confidence and took it for granted that people admire you. Acting confident will help you feel more confident.

"Call me next week and tell me how you are doing," I concluded.

She called from her office the very next day. "I can't do it," she said, her voice breaking. "I walked to work with my head up and shoulders back, but when I got in the elevator my boss was there and I felt so conspicuous . . . I slumped. I can't do it."

I sympathized. "I know it's hard, but you can do it. There is another psychological tool that will help you. Come by after work and I'll tell you how to use it."

## PREVISUALIZATION

Previsualization or Guided Imagery is a kind of mental rehearsal that can make Acting As If easier. You visualize what you will do and how you will do it—and then you go out and do it. Previsualization is more than wishful thinking. It is taking yourself mentally step by step through any challenging situation that confronts you.

Olympic Gold Medalist Dick Fosbury, who created a special high-jump technique, said that in his competition days, "I would psyche myself up, create a picture, 'feel' a successful jump—the perfect jump—and then develop a positive attitude to make the jump. My success came from the visualization and imaging process." What he had done was create a mental blueprint for what he would do in competition. Previsualization prepared his brain and body for the great effort he had to make for a winning jump.

Corporate heads use Previsualization when they are planning a takeover or considering launching a new product. Surgeons do a mental walk-through of an operation before they enter the operating room. The surgeon who performed the first successful separation of Siamese twins who were joined at the head spent five months Previsualizing every step of the twenty-two-hour operation.

When I spoke before a group of recently widowed and divorced women not too long ago, most questions were about going back to work, particularly about handling job interviews. I advised them to Previsualize the whole thing, from what they would wear to how confident they would feel during the interview and how effectively they would present their qualifications for the position. Several women wrote to tell me how helpful the mental rehearsal had been.

This advance role-playing yields positive results. The technique could not be simpler. Previsualizing just before you go to bed is most effective. The behavior seems to become established while you sleep.

1. Make yourself comfortable. Put your feet up or stretch out on your bed. Close your eyes and take deep slow breaths until you feel quiet and relaxed.

2. Now visualize whatever situation or behavior it is that confronts you. It may be an Acting As If situation or a speech you have to deliver or even walking down the aisle at your own

wedding. Whatever it is, visualize it step by step by step. If you are going to make a speech, picture yourself walking up to the podium, shaking hands with the master of ceremonies, taking a sip of the water on the podium, placing your hands on the podium, looking out at the audience. . . . Visualize everything, including the audience's applause.

3. Repeat the whole visualization process. Run it through your mind, as if you were viewing a film starring yourself. Don't omit a single step.

4. Go to bed and go to sleep. Your unconscious will be working for you. Whatever challenge you face tomorrow, you will handle competently. You will do better than if you had not Previsualized it.

## Anabel

I outlined the Previsualization technique for Anabel. "It will make you feel more comfortable about standing tall and acting confident when you go to work tomorrow."

"But I thought about walking into the office, standing tall, practically all last night," she protested. "It didn't help at all."

"You weren't thinking. You were dreading the idea and filling yourself full of anxiety. Tonight, you are going to Previsualize success. Start at the very beginning. See yourself looking in the mirror just before you leave for work. You will be standing straight, head high, looking yourself in the eye.

"Then see yourself walking to work. Walking into the building. Getting into the elevator. Some of your coworkers will be in the elevator. See yourself standing tall, smiling, saying 'Good morning,' leaving the elevator, walking down the hall, smiling and pleasant and completely at ease.

"Then go back to the beginning and visualize the whole thing over again. Concentrate on how relaxed and confident you will be. You will find it makes a difference. Call me next week," I said, "and let me know how you are doing."

"I did it," she reported the following week. "I thought it all out, made a mental movie out of it the way you said. And I managed to stick to it all week. It still scares me, though. I keep thinking people are staring at me and I want to hide."

This was a classic—and expected—reaction. Like all extremely shy people, she was so self-conscious that she felt everyone was watching and judging her. Because the shy are so concerned with themselves, they cannot conceive that others spend very little, if any, time thinking about them. I explained this and told Anabel that other people were nowhere near as observant as she was.

I suggested that she keep on Previsualizing and, in another week, start another Acting As If project. "You complained that you were lonely. The way to make friends is to reach out to people. You have to learn to talk to people. I suggest you do this by Acting As If talking with others was the most natural and pleasant thing in the world."

She groaned.

"All it takes is practice," I told her. "Start with nonthreatening, impersonal chitchat. Talk to the next person in line for movie tickets. Just smile and say, 'I've heard this is a marvelous film. The *Times* gave it a rave review.' Or start chatting while you're waiting in the checkout line at the supermarket. Say something like 'Can you believe the price of broccoli?' Talk to someone waiting in line at the bus stop. Or say something about the weather to someone in the elevator. Make yourself take the initiative once a day. People will respond, and you will find that talking to people becomes easier after a little practice.

"Then, once a week, ask someone in your office to have lunch."

"I won't know what to say," she protested.

"Use the same easy approach. Ask about her vacation or how she found her apartment or what she thinks about the company's medical plan. Ask her where she found those wonderful earrings. It will be easier than you think, and you will enjoy it."

"I doubt it," Anabel said, "but I'll try."

A month later, she called to say that she had lunched with several of the women in her office and that she had enjoyed it. "I feel more part of the group now that I know them better," she said. "And now *they* are asking *me* to lunch." She sounded delighted.

The Ripple Effect had started to work for her. I tell you about this self-generating phenomenon in the next chapter.

*Chapter Seven*

# THE SELF-GENERATED PHENOMENA

## The Ripple Effect and the Halo Effect

MOST PEOPLE ARE absolutely unaware of the existence of these two forces. Since they affect everyone's life, it is important to understand them.

The Ripple Effect will help you modify a self-defeating trait once you take the first step toward change. The Halo Effect can be positive or negative. If it is positive, it opens the door to success. If it is negative, you will have to work harder to reach your goals unless you can reverse its effect. The Ripple Effect is an ongoing force, while the Halo Effect has a limited life span.


THE RIPPLE EFFECT

This is an extraordinarily powerful mechanism of gradual change. The name hints at the far-reaching repercussions of even the smallest change. If you drop a pebble in a puddle after a rainstorm, you will see the ripples spread gently out and out and out, until they reach the edge. And so it is when you make a small change. There is a steady and controlled, calm and inevitable progression.

Major changes are different. They are like tossing a boulder into a swimming pool. You get a big splash. Things bounce up and down and bump against the sides of the pool. Major changes are always stressful and can be destructive. But small changes just ripple along quietly activating one little change after another.

One small change in behavior or attitude is all that is needed to trigger the Ripple Effect, setting the ripples into action, radiating out farther and farther, until eventually that change affects every aspect of your life. You may not even be aware of it until you look back and see how much you have changed.

And you never need to worry that the ripples of change may carry you too far, to the other extreme. The basic natural law of Reversion to the Mean will protect you and keep you close to the norm.

## Josie

Josie, the rust-belt executive, reaped the benefits of the Ripple Effect as she worked to control her temper. When I was in Chicago three months after my first interview with her, the CEO told me, "There has been a real change in that woman. Not that she's turned into a Girl Scout. But she's not called any of the other department heads a 'dumb ox' or told the men on the production line that they are 'lazy, fucking birdbrains' lately. And last week, when she and Ben—he's in charge of quality control—were butting heads together, she was the one who came up with a compromise."

"I still blow my top," Josie told me when we met. "But not as often. I don't need to. The people I work with are working harder and better than they used to."

"They responded to the change in you," I told her. "One change inevitably triggers another. As soon as you started to cut down on those temper outbursts, that change triggered changes in their behavior and attitudes. They no longer had to brace themselves against your anger. They no longer felt resentful or sullen. They felt more relaxed on the job. As a result, they are more efficient and productive."

"My management style was all wrong," she agreed. "Now I understand just how ineffective anger is as a motivator. When I got the production figures for this quarter—well, we beat our own record! And when one of the men came up with suggestions for speeding up a procedure so that we could do even better next quarter, I really knew that my efforts to control my temper were paying off."

Then she smiled, "Don't think I don't explode every now and then. I do. But when I do, I've thought it out first. I know what I want to achieve. These days when I pop off it shocks the hell out of them, because it's so unexpected."

Josie had succeeded in doing something that others might have thought impossible. She had turned her self-defeating trait into an asset.

## THE HALO EFFECT

The Halo Effect has nothing to do with saintliness. It is the result of the disproportionate effect of first impressions. If people meeting you for the first time consider you beautiful or amusing or charming (or, conversely, as unattractive or dull or snobbish), they will think of you this way in future meetings.

When it comes to first impressions, looks count. They count a lot. Appearance, not personality or behavior, is the most important determinant of the Halo Effect.

Studies have revealed that most people take it for granted that good-looking people have better jobs, higher salaries—and more fun. Unfair as it may seem, people believe that an attractive woman is more sensitive, more intelligent, more interesting, more exciting, even more worthwhile than a plain woman.

One study, carried out in connection with a college mixer

dance, underlined the impact good looks have on first impressions. The young men were told that their dates were being selected for them by a computer on the basis of shared interests, when there actually was no computer and they were paired off willy-nilly with women whom the researchers had secretly classified as attractive or unattractive. After the dance, each man was asked a series of questions designed to elicit how he liked his date and whether he planned to see her again. Shared interests, it turned out, had little to do with their estimation of their dates. The men who had been paired with attractive young women planned to see them again. Those whose dates had not been particularly attractive claimed that they had very little in common with them, and therefore did not plan to see them again.

Height produces a positive Halo Effect. Tall people are considered more intelligent and capable. People also believe that famous people are taller than average. When I am introduced to strangers as Dr. Brothers, they often do a double take, because I am only five-foot-two. Not so long ago, one woman even accused me of being an impostor. The real Dr. Joyce Brothers, she told me, was six feet tall.

The Halo Effect is not confined to personal appearance. It can be the first impression made by your telephone voice, your office stationery, even by the make of car you drive. If someone knows you are close to the President of the United States or the president of the country club, your Halo Effect is established sight unseen.

While the Ripple Effect is ongoing, the Halo Effect is instantaneous. I was particularly struck by a study in which psychologists, armed with stop watches, spent sixty nights in singles bars in order to find out how long it took a man to decide if a woman appealed to him. Seven seconds was all it took. If she did not strike him as attractive, he was off to another woman.

As you see, the Halo Effect can be deceptive—and unfair. First impressions, while important, are only first impressions. Nevertheless, a positive Halo Effect is an asset, a window of opportunity. It gets you off on the right foot and if you measure up to that first impression, you are on the way to reaching your goal in life, whatever it is.

If you don't measure up, a reaction eventually sets in as people realize you are not what they thought. A stunningly beautiful woman, for instance, may be self-centered and not terribly intelligent, but because of her looks, she creates a great first impression. As people get to know her, however, and realize how dull she is, they reverse their first impressions of her. And, more often than not, they go to the other extreme and consider her more self-centered and less intelligent than she really is.

A negative Halo Effect can be erased, but it takes time. Studies show that it takes seven to eight subsequent meetings to erase an unfavorable first impression. It took Anabel more than a year to completely erase her negative Halo Effect.

## Anabel

Anabel had been projecting a negative Halo Effect all her life. Her hunched, apologetic stance and her miserable shyness had broadcast the message, "I am not worth bothering about." When she began to stand tall and look the world in the eye, things began to change. Body language may be silent, but its message is loud and clear. Anabel now projected a message that "I am someone. I count." And then the Ripple Effect kicked in. As she continued Acting As If she was someone who counted, little by little people began to perceive her differently.

The first meaningful recognition of that change came a few months later when her boss gave her a small advertising account to supervise. "It's the first time he has given me this kind of responsibility," she said. "I've never worked with clients before." I assured her that she could handle anything a client tossed her way. I suspected that her boss had suddenly taken a fresh look at her, registered her new air of confidence and ease with people and realized he had been underestimating her abilities.

Two years later, she moved to a better-paid position in a larger, more prestigious advertising agency. While she is still quiet and self-contained, her Halo Effect is positive. She carries herself like a princess, dresses like a model and projects an air of self-assurance. Her demanding and often volatile clients see her as a confident and capable executive whose calm demeanor is reassuring.

*Part Three*

# ☑ SELF-ESTEEM DEFICITS
## You Were Not Born with Them

People with a self-esteem deficit have a self-defeating attitude toward life. If you are one of them, take comfort. You are not alone. Psychologists estimate that 85 percent of the population suffers from low or weak self-esteem, which is generally caused by a poor self-image.

To explain a subtle but significant difference, self-esteem is your good opinion of yourself, while self-image is your concept of yourself and your role in life. Self-image is the root of self-esteem. It is made up of many things—your abilities, achievements, job, family, sex life, economic status, social status, relationships with others, education and, especially for women, appearance. Low self-esteem reflects a low self-image.

No one is born with low self-esteem or a poor self-image. We acquire them, often because we have internalized other people's faulty perceptions of us. Or, our self-esteem can be diminished by our own faulty perceptions of ourselves—of our abilities and accomplishments, for instance, or our looks.

Whatever the cause of a person's low self-image, it is self-defeating and spawns self-defeating traits. In fact, these self-defeating traits are often the cause of the self-esteem deficit. It is like the chicken and the egg. Which came first? The self-defeating trait or the low self-esteem?

It does not really matter. What matters is that a poor self-image and self-defeating behaviors or beliefs go hand in hand. You may have a distorted image of yourself, be a compulsive spender, jealous, or sexually inhibited. Whatever it is, you can bring that undesirable behavior closer to the norm. You can improve your self-image and increase your self-esteem.

In this section, I suggest ways to change behaviors caused by low self-esteem, using some of the psychological tools I have outlined. There is a common pattern in this group of negative attitudes and behaviors, which means that the methods I suggest can be used to correct any self-defeating trait that stems from a self-esteem deficit.

# Chapter Eight

# SELF-DEFEATING SELF-IMAGES

## It May Not Be the Way You Look

THE MOST COMMON self-defeating self-image from which women suffer is the way they feel about the way they look. "We have established that the single most critical factor in self-esteem is physical appearance," says Dr. Susan Harter, professor of psychology at the University of Denver, who has researched this area.

It is not only what a woman sees in the mirror that establishes her self-image. The most important factors are how she believes she ought to look and what other people think of her looks. "Ideal body image is a social image," confirms Dr. April Fallon, a psychologist at the Medical College of Pennsylvania. "A woman is not only making a judgment about what she likes, but what other people think is appropriate or important."

Unfortunately the popular concept of beauty is both unrealistic and unattainable. Women come in many sizes and shapes, but when asked what they consider the ideal body, survey group after survey group replied that a woman should be around 5 feet 9 or 10 inches tall and weigh no more than 125 pounds.

Only a fraction of 1 percent of American women could ever hope to attain this string-bean ideal of beauty. According to the Census Bureau, only 3 percent of American women are 5 feet 9 inches or taller, and about one-third of them are overweight.

The 5-foot-9 woman who fits this ideal is some 15 to 20 pounds underweight. No wonder so many women have low self-esteem. As Gloria Steinem once said, "When we dislike our bodies, it is difficult to like ourselves."

But where did we get this unreal ideal of beauty? Not from real life, but from fashion magazines and advertising, with their dazzling photographs of incredibly thin models. "The whole business is deception," one model told the *New York Times*. "How can a five-foot-five woman with a pear-shaped body put on a pair of leather pants and a tight shirt, and look five-foot-ten, one hundred twenty pounds and toothpick thin? We give women false expectations, and we make them feel worse about themselves."

It is important to keep a sense of proportion. You may hate your looks, but are they self-defeating? Absolutely not. Yes, the Halo Effect governs first impressions. But you are *you*. In ninety-nine cases out of a hundred, the person who believes her looks are blocking her from the life she wants is wrong.

## DO A REALITY CHECK

Look at the women around you, the friends, neighbors and co-workers whom you consider attractive. How many of them fit that anorexic ideal? How many are cover-girl material? Few, if any. Real women have real looks and real bodies. One of the prettiest women I know is 5-foot-4 and a little pudgy. She has a hard time finding clothes that fit, but she has a glorious smile and a sweet face, and she seems to light up the room when she walks in.

And now look at yourself. Stand in front of a mirror and take a good look. How do you stack up against the others?

Better?
About the same?

Worse?

Much worse?

If you rate yourself "better" or "about the same," get back in front of that mirror and tell yourself, "There is nothing wrong with the way I look. I am going to change the way I feel about myself." There probably is something wrong, but it is not your looks and I suggest you make out a Basic Diagnostic List to find out just which psychological splinter is affecting your self-esteem.

If you rated yourself "worse" or "much worse," get back in front of that mirror and *Do a variation on the Diagnostic List*. Examine yourself carefully and write down your best and worst features from your hair to the nail of your little toe. You might come up with a list like this:

| Good Features | Bad Features |
| --- | --- |
| straight, narrow nose | hair, mousy and gray |
| good skin | eyes too close |
| full lips | crow's feet |
| ears, pretty | bags under eyes |
| good chin | deep laugh lines |
| neck okay | jawline, droopy |
| breasts okay | shoulders too narrow |

And so on, right down to your feet. Put the lists away overnight. Then study them and write down what you would change if you could. For instance, you might decide: "My hair can look better. I'm going to go to the best hairdresser in town for advice on color and cut. There is no way I can move my eyes wider apart, but perhaps makeup can make a difference. Next time I am in a department store, I'll ask at several of the cosmetic counters what they advise. Those bags under my eyes—are they really bad or am I being hypercritical? Perhaps I need to cut down on my alcohol intake or change my diet. I'll check with Dr. Jones. I could have plastic surgery. And that jawline, perhaps makeup can disguise the droop. I'll ask at the cosmetic counters when I ask about my eyes."

And so on, feature by feature. Do the same with your best features. When you have finished, ask yourself:

What bothers me most?

Can it be changed or disguised with makeup, exercise or diet?

Can it be changed with plastic surgery?


## TAKE ACTION

If exercise, diet or makeup can make a difference, start today. Put yourself on a healthy, low-fat diet. Join an exercise class and start a walking program. Tour the department-store cosmetic counters. Many of them offer complimentary makeovers. Tell them what you want your makeup to do for you and ask their advice.

If you feel that cosmetic surgery is the way to go, fine. But be realistic. No surgeon is going to turn you into a superbeauty. A good surgeon will refuse to accept you as a patient if she or he feels your expectations are too high. A surgeon will nip here and tuck there, and you will look ten years younger after you heal. But you will still be you.

Before you do anything about surgery, I recommend you do a Worst-Case Scenario—the worst that could happen if you had surgery; the worst that could happen if you did not. Consider the costs (high), the time, the pain, the temporary disfigurement, the fact that there is no such thing as surgery without risk. Balance the benefits you hope to gain against the drawbacks.

You now have a solid baseline to start thinking about what you want to do—if anything. You should think long and hard. Before you make up your mind, I want to point out some of the self-defeating aspects of changing one's appearance.

## YOUR LOOKS AND THE MAN IN YOUR LIFE

Great beauties often have difficulties in their relationships with men and many do not find lasting happiness in marriage. They tend to have low self-images and to be extremely insecure, since they come to believe that their looks are their only asset. And looks are obviously not enough, since in a recent survey, men agreed overwhelmingly that they preferred women who were reasonably attractive over stunning beauties.

A man will believe that his dumpy, dowdy wife is beautiful and chic. Handsome men marry women whose looks fall far short of beauty—and think them gorgeous. Extremely wealthy men have been known to have mistresses who could only be described as ugly—and to adore them. Dr. John Schimel, a psychiatrist associated with the William Alanson White Institute, insists that "There is no such thing as an ugly woman. Over the years," he says, "I have treated women who were, for instance, extremely overweight and yet were extraordinarily attractive to certain men who pursued them vigorously."

The reason for these diverse tastes is the secret-love profile that every man has encoded in his brain. It is based on perceptions of the earliest people in his life—parents, baby-sitters, playmates, relatives, neighbors. Long before adolescence, he has an unconscious but very definite idea of the woman of his dreams. His mother may have had wide hips. He may have had a baby-sitter who was freckled and whom he adored. His favorite aunt may have been blond. His kindergarten teacher may have had a receding chin. And the little girl he played with next door may have had a turned-up nose. So one day when he meets a freckled blonde with a turned-up nose, generous hips and a receding chin, he is bowled over.

Every man has his own inner picture of feminine beauty, and it may not coincide with yours. For instance, many women believe that men prefer big breasts. The fact is that while men may ogle women with highly developed bosoms, most men do not prefer large breasts. Researcher J. Kevin Thompson, a psychologist at the University of South Florida, has found that "what we believe society sets as its ideal in breast size is way out of line with reality."

When you consider that 120,000 women had breast implants for cosmetic reasons in 1990—the last full year before restrictions on the implants—it is obvious that thousands and thousands of women were spending a lot of money and putting themselves at risk because of the mistaken notion that bigger was better. Talk about self-defeating!

This all adds up to an important rule of thumb when you are considering cosmetic surgery. If you think it will make you more appealing to the man in your life, forget it. If he is turned off now, no physical makeover will turn him on again.

## THE SECONDARY GAIN TRAP

Many women who believe that their looks are denying them the love, admiration and success that they crave feel let down after a face-lift or other cosmetic surgery. They find that the surgery has improved their looks, but the self-esteem deficit still exists. So they try again and again and again, hoping that collagen injections, tummy tucks, nose jobs, liposuction or peels will finally make the difference. These women fall into what psychologists have labeled the Secondary Gain Trap, a very real danger lying in wait for women in search of beauty.

The Secondary Gain Trap is the substitution of the means for the end. When I was a student at Cornell, I was fascinated by an experiment in one of my laboratory courses. We put white mice in cages that had six or seven inches of sand on the bottom. There were containers of water on top of the sand, but no food. We buried the food under a thin layer of sand where the mice could smell it but not see it.

Digging is not a normal mouse activity, but the hungry mice

started scrabbling away in the sand to get at the food. We buried the food a little deeper every day until finally the mice had to dig down several inches for it. After a while, we stopped burying the food and put it on top of the sand.

The mice kept on digging. There was no reason for them to dig. Their food was right there, easily available. They were digging for the sake of digging. And they kept on digging until they died.

Just like the mice, some women get caught up in the process of physical self-improvement. They are never thin enough, blond enough, shapely enough. This is one area where the law of Reversion to the Mean does not protect from the extreme. Some women get so caught up in their desire to achieve perfection that their physical appearance becomes an obsession. No matter what they do, they never achieve their goal, because they have a distorted view of how they really look.

We have all heard bone-skinny women complaining about how grossly fat they are. They really believe it. As Judith Rodin, founder of Yale University's Eating Disorders Clinic, says, "Women are struggling with their self-image in part because the body component has the quality of quicksand."

This is one reason why I strongly recommend that any woman considering changing her looks do a Diagnostic List and a Worst-Case Scenario first. It clarifies your thinking about what really matters and why, and will keep you from falling into the Secondary Gain Trap.

## PSYCHOLOGICALLY SAFE MAKEOVERS

If, after consideration, you decide to have a face-lift because it will make you feel better about yourself or because looking a little better and a little younger will pay off in your career, then go for it. In the same way, if you worry that your gray hair is a negative career factor since people place such a premium on youth, or if you feel depressed every time you see that gray-haired woman in the mirror, go ahead, color your hair. I intend to be blond forever.

Face-lifts and hair coloring are what I consider psychologically safe makeovers. I call them "psychologically safe" because they make you feel better about yourself and are unlikely to upset the man in your life.

You have to understand something about men. Most share a wonderful and endearing trait. No matter how many years have passed, they still see you as the girl they fell in love with. Oh, he sees the streaks of gray and the crow's-feet, but in his mind's eye, you are still twenty-two. If you were pigeon plump then or had an A-cup profile or pudgy thighs, he loved the way you looked. And to him, you still look the same.

Once when I was putting on weight, I asked my husband, who was a physician, if he had any suggestions for an easy way to lose weight. I must confess that I had just polished off two helpings of chocolate mousse with whipped cream.

"For starters," Milt said, "you might try limiting yourself to one helping of dessert. But you don't need to lose weight. You look fine." This is what they mean when they say love is blind.

If a man runs into an old girlfriend he has not seen for twenty years, he thinks to himself, "She's really showing her age." But the same twenty years have made no difference in the way you look to him. Not only have the changes been gradual, but he has an inner censor that does not allow him to notice the changes, because he wants to see you just as you were.

So if you color your hair or have a face-lift, it is psychologically safe. He will take it in stride, because it brings you closer to that picture he has in his mind's eye of the way you looked when he first met you. He may even say that he doesn't see why you went to all that expense and effort, you look just the same. Men really are dear.

## PSYCHOLOGICALLY RISKY MAKEOVERS

But there are other changes that your significant other *will* notice—and he may not like them. A breast reduction, for instance, or the loss of thirty pounds or a nose job. These are real changes. That is not the nose he always adored. Or the pigeon-plump figure that turned him on.

It is important to think twice before making this kind of alteration in your appearance, because it may turn out that what you corrected was what he adored about you. Sometimes you just don't know what the man in your life likes about your looks. I have done my share of self-remodeling and I know what I am talking about.

I have worn glasses ever since first grade. When contacts became available, I was thrilled. But when I got my first contacts, my husband looked at me and said I looked better with glasses. I did not agree, but forever after I wore my glasses when he was home and kept my contacts for public appearances.

And then there were my teeth. When I was young my front teeth were quite protuberant. My folks thought I looked cute. "Like a little bunny," my dad used to say. But I hated the way they made me look.

When I began to earn my own money, I saved until I had enough for the orthodontist. I wore braces for months back when it was unheard of for a young married woman to be running around with a mouth full of wires. I considered the end result a great improvement, well worth the money and the discomfort, although I still bore a slight resemblance to a bunny.

But Milt was disappointed. It turned out that the bunny look was one of the things that he found enchanting about me. I could not believe it. I really thought I looked much better, but just recently I came across some research showing that some men are turned on sexually by women with slightly protruding front teeth. So you never know.

The message is that we often are not aware of what it is about us that appeals to the people who love us. The feature that a woman considers a flaw may be the very thing that brings her love and makes her unique.

Study after study has shown that we do not see ourselves as others see us. In one study the participants were asked to look at themselves in a three-way mirror and tell the researcher what they considered their best and worst features. Then they asked each woman's significant other what he thought. Almost invariably the thing that a woman liked least about herself was the very feature that her significant other found most lovable.

It may be that women's dissatisfaction with their looks is simply a persistent remnant of the bygone age when beauty was a survival tool. Professors Robin Lakoff and Raquel Scherr point out that in past centuries "women used beauty to gain power or whatever they could gain, but they were also used by beauty." Once their beauty faded, their husbands and lovers looked elsewhere, and the power went to younger women.

In some circles, this is still true, though changing rapidly. Women have discovered they have other strengths that are more effective than beauty. A recent series of studies by psychologist Stephen Franzoi at Marquette University established that women who are traditionally feminine, compliant and nurturing tend to be unhappy with their bodies and want to change them. But women who pride themselves on their intelligence, courage and drive as well as on their empathic and nurturing qualities are happier with their appearance and score much higher on tests of body-esteem. They do not fall into the cultural trap of judging their looks by the way they believe others judge them.

## SUMMING UP

Self-esteem, when all is said and done, comes from within. If it is love and admiration and success you are seeking, then courage and drive combined with warmth and humor are more effective ways to get them than any amount of surgical tinkering.

But what if you are not all that brave and energetic? The answer is quite simple. Use that wonderful psychological tool—Acting As If. Act As If you were courageous and energetic. What if you lack warmth and humor? Again, Act As If you were warm and witty. Chances are that you have every one of these qualities, but have not been using them. By Acting As If, you will liberate them, and they will liberate you—and boost your self-esteem.

As for the way you look, by now you know the answer. If you Act As If you were attractive, people will perceive you that way. This is why cosmetic surgery is so effective for many women. Basically, the surgeon excises the droops and the flab, with the result that you look younger. Yet there is no magic. You are not transformed, but you feel so good about yourself that unconsciously you Act As If you look great. A woman who Acts As If will never fall into the Secondary Gain Trap.

Remember when your mother told you that beauty comes from within? She was right. You just have to let it out.

*Chapter Nine*

# THE PASSIVITY TRAP

Free Yourself to Be the Woman You Can Be

SELF-IMAGE IS not simply a matter of looks. The most damaging kind of self-image may be the result of underestimating yourself, of not letting yourself be all that you *could* be. Too many women go through life being less than their best because of a negative self-image. They do not believe that they are valuable.

The result is that they become passive and accept whatever life brings their way, because they do not believe they can do anything about it. "If my husband knocks me around when he's been drinking, that's the way he is. . . . If he says we can't afford to let Gail have piano lessons, well that's the way . . ." These women are captives of passivity. Since they have never taken the initiative, they believe they are incapable of changing anything about their lives. And there are more women who are prisoners of their own passive outlook on life than you might believe.

Working women tend to have higher self-esteem than women who stay home and run households and raise children. Not because they are doing something more worthwhile, but because every day, they must make decisions and take actions and are able to rate themselves against other people.

When a woman who has always been at home has to face life on her own, she may have no idea of what to do. It is not that she lacks intelligence, but that she has never asserted herself. These prisoners of passivity start out with an abysmal self-image. Like Carol, they have to learn how it feels to have a solid self-esteem. It is something like having to learn how to walk all over again.

It took Carol a long time to understand that she had power over her own life. She was the middle child in her family, wearing her older sister's hand-me-downs. Her younger brother was coddled and adored. She was lost someplace in between. At nineteen, she married a man she had dated for only three months, more because she wanted a home of her own rather than because she was in love.

At fifty, she emerged from a divorce, menopausal, wearied by the emotional turmoil, fearful of being on her own and next door to impoverished, since her former husband's modest salary could not stretch to more than a "minimum-wage" alimony. She did not know what to do with herself. She had always thought of herself as a wife and homemaker.

## A FAR FROM GAY DIVORCÉE

Carol spent most of her days watching television, retreating into a couch-potato passivity. This lasted until the day, four months after the divorce, when the bank informed her that her checking account was overdrawn. Her husband had always handled the money and paid the bills. She had never realized the importance of filling in the stubs of her checkbook. For the first time, it hit home that her alimony was not enough to live on.

She had no skills and no experience, but she had more common sense than she gave herself credit for. The supermarket displayed HELP WANTED signs for checkout clerks. She hated the idea, because everyone would see her and know she had no money and feel sorry for her. But what else could she do?

She applied for a job, expecting to be turned down. To her

surprise, she was hired immediately. The first two weeks were torture. Her feet hurt. Her arms and shoulders ached from lifting and bagging. Her head was whirling with all the new knowledge about the cash register, and weighing things and coping with coupons. Still, she was grateful to be earning money.

A few months later, she spent some of the money to attend a lecture I gave in a neighboring city. She had dithered about going, but, as she wrote me later, "I had never seen a real-life celebrity in person. I'd seen you on TV and I decided this was my chance." The Ripple Effect had already set in. Six months earlier she would never have dreamed of taking such an initiative. I spoke about reinventing oneself and the psychological tools one could use. "It was like a sign," she said. "I knew it was what I should do." And she went to work to reinvent herself.

## THE WOMAN SHE WAS MEANT TO BE

If you are not the person you want to be, you can turn yourself into the person you were meant to be. This does not mean that you can be the president of the New York Stock Exchange or an Academy Award winner or editor of *Good Housekeeping*, although things just might turn out that way. But you can definitely become a woman who feels good about herself, a woman with a strong self-image and high self-esteem, a woman who is in charge of her life.

I had made this clear in the lecture Carol had attended. And she grabbed at the idea. She had made enormous strides since she had started working. She was more confident, enjoyed the snatches of conversation at the checkout counter, and had lost nearly ten pounds now that she was no longer sitting around watching television all day.

Her first step was to make a Basic Diagnostic List. I recommend making the following two changes in the list if you are using it as a guide to reinventing yourself.

1. List your *six* best qualities.
2. List your three greatest achievements, the three things that you are most proud of, instead of your three worst qualities. This variation of the Diagnostic List is a feel-good exercise, Positive Reinforcement for your self-image. This is a time to concentrate on your assets.
3. And, of course, list your three chief goals in life. There is something almost magical about writing down your goals. People who write down their goals tend to reach them more often and sooner than people who do not. Putting a goal down on paper makes it more real, more attainable.

When it comes to writing down your goals, reach for the stars. What goals do you fantasize about when you daydream? High expectations have a way of becoming realities. Aim at becoming the best of what you want to be. Take the full six weeks to work on your list. You are seeking the real inner you, and she may be buried deep down.

Carol's list of her six best qualities read like this:

1. Good housekeeper
2. Honest
3. I love children even though I could never have any.
4. Dependable
5. Hard worker. After working at the checkout counter in the supermarket, I'm convinced I can do almost anything.
6. Self-reliant, at least more than I used to be. I've learned how to manage my money. And I found myself a job.

The hardest thing for Carol was coming up with three achievements she was proud of. She really had to search her mind. The idea of being proud of something she had done was foreign to her. She finally listed:

1. Getting and keeping my job at the supermarket. It was the first job I ever had.
2. Coping with being divorced.
3. Being named Easiest-to-Get-Along-With in my high school yearbook.

This woman who had never set a goal for herself in her life now had no trouble at all in listing her goals.

1. Making more money so I can stay in my house.
2. Making some new friends.
3. Finding a better job.

She made copies of her lists and stuck one on the refrigerator door, another on the bathroom mirror and put one on her bedside table. She studied them every day. They represented six weeks of introspection, of hard thinking. Then she started a list of her own—a list of ways to reach her goals. She listed everything she could think of from selling real estate to getting married again. Then she narrowed it down to two possibilities.

1. I could be a housekeeper for a working couple. I have plenty of experience keeping house. I'm honest and dependable. But it might be lonely—all alone all day in someone else's house.
2. I could take in boarders. Two or three. But I am not sure I feel comfortable with the idea of living with strangers under my roof.

At that time, the Zoe Baird case started making headlines, and Baird withdrew her name for consideration for U.S. Attorney

General because of the reaction to the fact that she had employed an illegal alien to care for her son. The episode threw a spotlight on the very serious problem of finding quality day care for the children of working mothers.

## THE TIME COMES WHEN THINGS FALL INTO PLACE

As she watched the television coverage, Carol was surprised at the substantial sums that parents were willing to pay for responsible child-care. Then lightning struck. "I could do this!" she told herself excitedly. She had a house with a big fenced-in backyard. She loved children, had plenty of room and people needed help. It was the answer. She could take five or six pre-schoolers.

Two weeks later, she was down in the dumps. She had discovered that the requirements for such a center were very stringent in her town, but she decided to go ahead. She enrolled in an evening child-care course at the community college. On weekends, she painted and childproofed the first floor of her house and haunted tag sales looking for child-size tables and chairs. She found a second-hand playpen and a crib in the thrift shop. Everything had to be cleaned and painted. She slip-covered foam slabs that would double as nap-time mattresses and play mats.

A year later, she was ready. She posted a notice on the supermarket bulletin board and put an ad in the local paper. The child-care instructor recommended her to several people. Within a week, five children, ranging from six months to three years, were signed up. She was in business.

It had been a hectic year. She had worked a lot of extra hours at the supermarket to pay for the thrift-shop furnishings and the paint and the vinyl floor she had put down in the former living room and dining room. She had spent hundreds of hours painting, sewing, planning and studying.

## A NEW WOMAN AND A NEW LIFE

Carol had reinvented herself. She had reached her goals. She had new friends. She was supporting herself doing something she really wanted to do.

She had also been Acting As If for months without knowing it. Acting As If she were an experienced, competent businesswoman, she had educated herself in the latest child-care techniques and concepts, coped with all the paperwork, remodeled the first floor of her house into a bright and cheerful set of rooms just right for small children.

She had transformed an idea into a reality. And she looked ten years younger. The passivity that had characterized her for so many years had disappeared. She had released her inner self—the energetic, happy, take-charge woman who had been suppressed for most of her life.

Why had she sold herself short? Why had she let her family cast her as the insignificant one? Why had she sentenced herself to the lonely life of a homemaker with no outside interests? There could have been a dozen reasons and there probably were, but they do not matter. What matters is that Carol was able to become the woman she was meant to be, the woman she *wanted* to be. Her self-esteem deficit is a thing of the past.

You may not want to be a big-time CEO or even a small-time executive. Perhaps what you really want most is to feel good about yourself, that you are a valuable and interesting person whom others want to know better. You want to stop standing in your own way. You want to get rid of your self-defeating self-image.

In the previous chapter, I discussed ways to improve the outer you, the physical you. But the inner you is far more important. As I said, you can look like a *Vogue* model and still have a poor self-image.

It is the inner you that governs your perception of yourself. When I talk about reinventing yourself, I do not mean making a change that turns you into someone you are not. The change you want to make is to release the real you so your life will be happier and more fulfilling.

# Chapter Ten

# PERFECTIONISM

---

## The Impossible Dream That Destroys Your Self-Esteem

---

It is April 15 and Hilda is frantically looking for the material she needs to make out her income tax, which must be mailed before midnight.

"I'm a terrible procrastinator," Hilda tells herself. "I put things off till the last moment and end up driving myself crazy."

It is two o'clock in the morning and Dottie still has not finished the report she must present to the School Board at noon. This is her fifth draft and while it is good enough, it is not as good as she thinks it should be. She rips it up and starts again.

"I'm a terrible procrastinator," Dottie tells herself. "I put things off till the last moment and end up driving myself crazy."

One of these women is a procrastinator; the other is not. If, like Hilda, you often find yourself putting off doing things you dislike until the very last moment, you are a procrastinator. But if, like Dottie, you often find yourself doing something over and over again because it is not good enough, you are *not* a procrastinator. You are something else again. You are a perfectionist.

Everyone procrastinates from time to time, putting off un-wanted tasks like balancing the checkbook or writing a thank-you note for that ghastly tea cozy Aunt Tillie sent for your birthday. It is a mildly self-defeating behavior. You may want to do something about it before your checking account is over-drawn, or Aunt Tillie cuts you out of her will.

Perfectionism is different. It sounds admirable, but it can block you from achievement, from recognizing your abilities and talents, and batter your self-esteem. Perfectionism is an im-possible dream. Unattainable. No matter how hard you try, you will never do as well as you think you should.

Nevertheless, if you are a perfectionist, you should not try to exorcise the trait. That would be a truly self-defeating endeavor, because it is impossible. All you want to do is bring your perfec-tionism into balance.

I start out with this warning because the perfectionist tends to have an either-or approach. "I'll do this perfectly or die in the attempt." Of course, she does neither. All that happens is that she feels inadequate, because once again, she has failed to achieve perfection.

## THE PERFECT APPLE PIE

Just think about perfection for a moment. Is there such a thing as a perfect apple pie? The combination of spices may be superb, but the apples are a bit bland. And some of the apple slices may be uneven. The pastry is all right, but it could be flakier and richer. The fluting around the edges is uneven. But that apple pie is delicious and everyone wants seconds.

It may not have been perfect, but it was good enough. And because you did not fool around all afternoon worrying about each and every detail, you were able to make it and bake it and serve it. What more could you want? Or expect? If, by chance, you had made the perfect apple pie (whatever that might be), what would you do next time? Could you ever duplicate that masterpiece? Does it matter?

## THE PERFECTIONIST PATTERN

The perfectionist pattern is clear. You know what you have to do. You look forward to doing it. You think about it. You know that you can do a good job, but good is not enough. You want it to be perfect.

Almost everyone has a touch of perfectionism. My mother-in-law once ripped out the last twenty-six rows of a sweater with a complicated pattern that she was knitting for my husband, because she had discovered a twisted stitch in the twenty-seventh row. No one except my mother-in-law would ever have spotted it. This kind of perfectionism is harmless unless you are knitting sweaters for a living, in which case it would be extremely self-defeating.

The self-defeating perfectionist takes one of two roads when faced with a project or an assignment. She may do nothing about it until the last minute. This is an unconscious way of providing herself with an excuse. "I just didn't have time to do a really good job," she says. The result is that she never does justice to herself or her abilities. People are disappointed and annoyed at what they consider slipshod, incompetent work. They feel she has failed and so does she.

Or she may deliver it on time, but have devoted more time to it than necessary. Even though people are delighted with the fine job she did and tell her so, she is not satisfied with the result, because doing a good job is simply not good enough for a perfectionist.

Dr. Steven J. Hendlin, a clinical psychologist and author, calls this "never-enough thinking." He tells his patients that "Perfection is a fantasy."

The perfectionist who understands this has made the first

small, but very important, step toward change. Most people want to do things well. They strive for excellence—in everything from parallel parking to toilet training to placing a satellite in orbit. But excellence is not enough for the perfectionist. The car must be perfectly aligned two inches from the curb. Baby should be completely toilet trained at twelve months. The satellite must be placed in perfect orbit—none of that nonsense of tweaking it about later to put it in the desired orbit.

In their striving for perfection, they often fall short of excellence. Even worse, they lose the joy of accomplishment, which makes them double losers. They cut themselves off from the satisfaction of accomplishment and each time they fail to reach perfection, their self-image becomes weaker.

But how do you move this perfectionist trait closer to the norm? *There are three preliminary steps:*

1. Recognize that, as Dr. Hendlin says, "Perfection is a fantasy."
2. Recognize that perfectionism is a self-defeating characteristic.
3. Decide that you will aim for excellence instead of perfection, and try to understand that "good enough" is good enough.

It is not enough to just read these words and tell yourself, "Yes, that is what I will do." *Turn them into Positive Reinforcements:*

1. Write them down. Use your own words, perhaps something like, "Perfectionism is an impossible dream. I know that. . . . My perfectionism is self-defeating. . . . From now on, I will strive for excellence and be satisfied with the 'good enough.' "

2. Then read what you have written out loud in front of a mirror.

Helen developed her own version of these three steps once she realized just how self-defeating her perfectionist behavior was. But it took a shock to make her understand that her perfectionism was standing in the way of success.

## THE PERFECTIONIST TRAP

"I'll never get it done," Helen said as she stared at the stacks of paper on her desk. A month ago her boss had asked her to prepare a report on the merits of three health-management groups that the company was considering. It was the biggest responsibility he had ever given her, but well within her capabilities. As his assistant she had helped him prepare many reports on employee benefits. There was no reason why she could not handle this one on her own.

The material had been on her desk for two weeks and was due tomorrow. But she had not written word one. She worked on it until three in the morning, and late in the afternoon she handed it to her boss. "I'm sorry it's not better," she said, "but I just could not get to it until the last minute."

The next day her boss asked her for the material she had used to prepare the report. "Your analysis left out a number of key factors," he said. "I'm going to work on it myself before I present it to the board."

A few weeks later she inadvertently (or had he left it out on purpose?) saw his comments on her annual review. She was shaken. "No follow-through," it read. "Can't handle responsibility. Disorganized."

She spent a sleepless night. "He's right," she thought. "I'm always waiting until I can do a job properly, but the time never comes. And when I do get to it, I never have time to do a decent job." The next day, she went off to work, full of good resolutions, but somehow they dissipated into thin air.

The needed impetus to change was supplied by a magazine article on perfectionism. It was one of those "Aha!" moments when things suddenly become clear. She fit the description of a perfectionist almost down to the last dotted *i* and crossed *t*.

She craved approval. She was so desirous of doing things perfectly that she put off doing them until the last minute. Then, if they were not done perfectly, it would not be her fault. It would simply be that she had not had enough time to do whatever it was.

The twisted logic of this behavior was embarrassingly familiar. She decided that she would never be guilty of this kind of thinking again—a true perfectionist approach. The perfectionist tends to go to extremes—and her belief that she could yank perfectionism completely out of her personality was extreme.

But in this case, she turned her belief into a very useful psychological tool. She concentrated on Acting As If she were not a perfectionist.

She started with the office files. She had been meaning to straighten them out for months, but had been waiting to find a block of time when she could make a perfect job of it. Now she stayed an hour late every day, making decisions on what went where faster than she had ever done in her life. She no longer tortured herself trying to decide which file a document belonged in. If there was any doubt, she simply photocopied it and placed it in both files.

Eventually, she turned chaos into order. She also came up with a project that she hoped would make her boss change his opinion of her. She decided to analyze productivity in the context of work hours, numbers of employees, salaries, output and quality. All the necessary information was at her fingertips in the files. It had never been pulled together.

She would also do some outside research, she thought, get supporting figures from other companies with a predominantly white-collar staff so that the report would have more depth. That would take time, of course. Probably months, since no other business would allow her similar access to their files.

Suddenly, she realized that she was falling into the perfectionist trap again. The important thing was to type up her findings about her own company, with appropriate charts, and give the material to her boss. *As soon as possible.*

Helen was able to halt her reversion to perfectionism as soon as she was aware of it. But other perfectionists may need a little more ammunition against the enemy. If you should find it difficult to repress your perfectionist behavior, there is a form of Negative Reinforcement that is particularly effective. When you catch yourself falling into the perfectionist trap, stop what you are doing. Grab a pencil and paper and write down why you believed this perfectionist behavior or approach was necessary and what would happen if you did not do it.

Don't just think it out—write it down. You are trying to establish a new behavior pattern, and writing is one way of reinforcing a behavior. Once you have thought through what you were doing and realized that the perfectionist approach would have made little or no difference to the ultimate result, you have reinforced your good-enough thinking as opposed to your perfectionist thinking.

But back to Helen. She continued her Acting As If behavior and went to work on the project immediately. It was exciting when she saw a trend developing of higher salaries and fewer employes equalling fewer work hours and higher productivity. The caliber of the employee was the key factor.

A week later, it was on her boss's desk with a memo. "This material on productivity has never been pulled together. I thought it would interest you in view of the recent discussions about overhead."

He found it both useful and challenging. It was a new way for the company to look at an old problem. She mentioned another area that had struck her as she had caught up with her filing—

the cumulative costs of pension payouts and ways to increase the money accumulated by the pension funds.

"Go to it," he told her.

A few months later, he called her into his office. "I'm moving upstairs," he said. "They've made me a vice president. How would you feel about taking over the department?"

## GOOD ENOUGH IS REALLY GOOD ENOUGH

Helen had taken a disciplined approach toward modifying her behavior, and both the actions she took—organizing the files and writing an imaginative and challenging report—gave her megadoses of Positive Reinforcement and the solid satisfaction of accomplishment. She received more Positive Reinforcement when her boss encouraged her to take on the second project. She was able to modify her perfectionism so that it was no longer self-defeating and has learned that good enough is truly good enough and far more rewarding than the impossible goal of perfectionism.

This is all you need ask of yourself—to do whatever it is well enough to accomplish its purpose. Let yourself experience the joy of accomplishment as Helen did. You will feel better about yourself. You will no longer be standing in your own way. You will have changed a self-defeating trait into a true asset.

# Chapter Eleven

# PROCRASTINATION

---

## A Kind of Self-Sabotage

---

UNLIKE PERFECTIONISTS, PROCRASTINATORS are incorrigible opti-
mists. They operate under the assumption that if you postpone
things you don't want to do long enough, they eventually go
away. And many of them do. Unfortunately some of the things
the procrastinator did not get around to doing may have been
the opportunities of a lifetime. The procrastinator usually never
knows what might have been. Anne learned the hard way.

The boss's secretary called Anne on Saturday morning, leaving a message on the answering machine, asking her to return
the call. She said it was important. Anne got the message, but
didn't return the call. Whatever it was, it could wait until Monday.

When she walked into the office on Monday, she discovered
that the boss had been taken ill and Cassie had flown to Dallas
on Saturday to take the boss's place at the annual Widget &
Sprocket Convention. "We called you first," the secretary said,
"but I guess you were away for the weekend."

When Cassie returned, she wrote a detailed report on what
had gone on, the people she had met and suggestions for new
products, based on what she had learned about their competi-
tors' plans. A few months later, Cassie was made a vice presi-

dent. The way she had represented the firm in Dallas and her suggestions for new products had put her in the spotlight.

Anne was left with a load of "if only" guilt. For months she went around thinking "If only I had returned that call, I might have made vice president. I certainly would have done as well as Cassie." Not every unanswered telephone call is a now-or-never opportunity, but procrastinators may never know when opportunity knocked. They soon become known for what they are. People stop giving them important assignments and asking them to join committees. Procrastinators are tagged as unreliable.

Procrastination is easy enough to remedy if you are motivated. If you have had enough of rushing at the last minute or if you realize that people think of you as someone who cannot be relied on to follow through, there are three psychological tools that can help you curb your tendency to postpone—a variation on the Reinforcement List, a Worst-Case Scenario and generous amounts of Positive Reinforcement.


## GETTING STARTED

The great thing about most of my psychological tools is that they can be adapted to almost any behavior. In this case, the Reinforcement List is really a Procrastination List. Start by listing everything that you put off till the last minute, including those things that you never did get around to. The list should include all those chores like cleaning the bathroom, sewing on buttons, making out your expense account, calling your mother, writing that thank-you note, picking up the stuff from the cleaner's, planning your daughter's birthday party, typing up your notes on the library board meeting. It will probably seem endless.

The next step is to organize your Procrastination List in order of importance. You may run into problems here trying to weigh whether balancing your checkbook should come before paying the dentist. (Balance the checkbook first. You don't want your check to bounce.) If you are unsure of your priorities, take the time to work out Worst-Case Scenarios. Suppose, for instance, your list included

- paying the rent
- paying the credit-card bill
- calling Joan to see if she and her husband can come to dinner a week from Friday
- making an appointment at the hairdresser's
- signing up for the dog obedience class
- taking the kids' outgrown clothes to the thrift shop

and you can't decide what you should do first. Just think of the worst that could happen if you did not get around to doing each of them. Then base your priorities on this, scheduling the tasks in order of the severity of the penalty for not doing it. For instance, the worst that might happen if you did not pay the rent could be a communication from the landlord's lawyer or even the cancellation of your lease. If you don't pay your charge-card bill, you will be charged more interest, your credit rating may be affected, and your card may be canceled, depending on your record. This is obviously a priority, but the rent has a higher priority. After all, you need a roof over your head.

The dinner invitation should probably be next if you want Joan and her husband to come. If you delay asking her, they may have made other plans. As for the hairdresser, the dog obedience class and the thrift shop, fit these in when you have time.

Now that you have an idea of the extent of the task that you face, set a goal. A reasonable one might be that every day you will take care of the three top items on your list. You might also set a secondary goal—you will never again postpone doing the items in the first half of your list. If you slip occasionally—and you may—just forgive yourself and keep on working toward your goal.

There are little tricks you can use to get started. Circle the days when something should be done on your calendar. Write down the chore and the due date on several index cards and tape them to the refrigerator, the bathroom mirror, next to the telephone, inside the front door, places where you will not be able to miss them, so that you cannot say that you simply forgot to take the car for an emissions test or to make an appointment with the gynecologist or to return your library books. And then do it.

## MY OWN TO-DO SYSTEM

I have had to fight against my own tendency to procrastinate, and over the years I have devised a system of priorities that works for me. I have three "To Do" baskets in my office and I put things in them depending on their degree of importance.

The first basket is for things that absolutely must be done today, the emergencies of my professional and family life, such as letters that must be answered, calls that must be returned, plane reservations that must be made, appointments that must be kept, a lecture that must be prepared, a birthday chat with one of my grandchildren, a television appearance—that sort of thing.

I start off every morning by sitting down and deciding what three things I absolutely must do today, the things that will make a difference. And I do them immediately. I can't always complete them. I call someone and he is not in his office. I order a book and it is out of stock. But I have taken a step. Once you have taken the first step you are on your way.

I never go to bed without taking care of the contents of the first basket. I am usually able to finish those duties by the middle of the afternoon unless I am out of town. And when I am, the contents of that basket travel with me. I take care of as much as I can from my hotel room wherever I am.

When that basket is empty, I get my reward, my Positive Reinforcement, the satisfaction of accomplishment. There is absolutely nothing like it. When I know that I have taken care of the obligations and crises of the first basket, I feel great. I often give myself a double-dip reward. I take time out and go for a walk or a swim in the apartment-house pool, or spend half an hour on the telephone visiting with my daughter. The break energizes me for the rest of the day.

The second basket is for after the emergencies have been taken care of—appointments that must be made, paying bills, writing my columns and books, shopping, reading, the hairdresser. This basket is always overflowing.

Most days I am able to make a start on the second basket. Before I go to bed at night, I review its contents, move some of them into the first basket and leave the rest where they are.

The third basket, a large laundry basket, is for everything else. I get to it when I can. At the end of each year, I go through it to check if there is still life in anything there and throw the rest out. Often there are things that I wish I could have done, and I regret that I did not get to them, but it does not matter. What matters is that all year long I do the things that really make a difference today, tomorrow and the next day.

## THE GLORIOUS SENSE OF ACCOMPLISHMENT

The Procrastination List is an extremely effective way of establishing the habit of doing things when they should be done. The making of this list is a chore you should not allow yourself to postpone. Once a week, make a list of everything you accomplished on time that week. When you have finished your list, sit back and congratulate yourself. It's a good feeling. But don't leave it at that. Give yourself a little more Positive Reinforcement—a treat of some sort, a little indulgence—and tell yourself you have earned it.

Positive Reinforcement is important. The process of modifying a behavior should be as rewarding as possible. I do not mean that you should buy yourself a string of pearls every month you pay the electric bill on time, but do treat yourself to some small delight.

One way to get things done and reward yourself at the same time is to do the thing you most dislike first. For each detested task you complete, allow yourself to tackle one you enjoy or that is easy. If you got the newsletter for your local Audubon Society group out on time, reward yourself by doing the least unpleasant chore on your list. Then tackle the next detested job.

Your Procrastination List will be a record of your progress from week to week. I suggest keeping it up for eight to ten weeks. By that time, the habit of doing what has to be done when it should be done should be well established.

Do not let yourself think you are a failure if you still procrastinate now and then. No one expects you to be perfect.

*Chapter Twelve*

# THE SPENDING TRAP

## What Money Can't Buy

MONEY IS A fantastically powerful force, a symbol, the way we keep score. We spend more time thinking about money than about sex, our families, our jobs, politics or food. It may be the last taboo. We guard the secret of our wealth or lack of it the way nations guard their nuclear weapons. People who will happily discuss their sex lives clam up when it comes to their incomes, concealing how much they earn from family and friends. Five percent of married women don't even let their husbands know how much they make. People work for it, scheme for it, even kill for it.

But money is not omnipotent. When all is said and done, it is simply a means to an end. And those ends are limited. But the power of money is such that some people mistakenly believe it can fulfill their emotional needs, supply what is lacking in their inner lives and cancel their self-esteem deficits. They believe that if they had enough money, they would be happy. These beliefs are self-defeating and lead to trouble, because money can do none of these things.

To a limited extent, money can buy a degree of happiness. Most people with an income of $50,000 a year are happier than most people with $25,000. And much happier than most of those with only $15,000. But—people with $100,000 or even $1,000,000 a year are no happier than those with $50,000. For example, once the initial euphoria has dissipated, lottery winners who have become rich beyond their wildest dreams are no happier and usually much less happy than they were before.


## THE PREPOTENT NEEDS

The happiness that money can bring is limited by our prepotent needs. These needs are the rock-bottom basic essentials for life. They are air, mothering, water, food and sex. In that order. Their relative importance was established by a landmark study that has been repeated by generations of science students.

A rat is put in a box that is separated from another box by an electrified grid that will give the rat a shock if it so much as touches a paw to it. Then the air is removed from the rat's box. The number and intensity of shocks that the rat will sustain in its mad scramble across the grid to get out of the airless box and into the other one are measured.

If the rat is hungry, food is placed in the second box; if the rat is thirsty, water. If the rat has just given birth, her pups will be put in the second box. If the sexual drive is being tested, a male is placed in the first box and a female in heat in the other.

Rats will suffer the most and strongest shocks to get to the box with air. They will undergo almost as many shocks to get to their pups. After air and mothering, the number of shocks they will endure diminishes progressively from water to food to sex.

Not every animal research finding applies to humans, but the prepotent needs are elemental and universal. They shape our actions more than we realize. In our civilization, money has become a substitute gratification for some prepotent needs. Money buys the food we need. Money permits us to feed and shelter and otherwise nurture our children. Most of us have to work for that money. We have to be dressed appropriately for whatever it is we do. We have to have transportation to get us to the place we work. Money is the enabler, the substitute gratification, that allows us to fulfill our prepotent needs. The upshot is that we tend to believe that money is the source of well-being and happiness.

Once we have met our prepotent needs, we can go on to satisfy our self-actualization needs—the psychologists' term for what we really want in life. We can study medicine, plant an orchard, run for Congress, play the violin, take the kids to Disneyland, read a novel.

But money is not a substitute gratification for our emotional needs. Money cannot be happy for you when you get that promotion. Money cannot console you when your son dies. Money cannot comfort you when you are ill and afraid. Money cannot laugh with you. Money cannot hold your hand in the moonlight. It cannot buy love or assuage loneliness. We have to fill these needs ourselves with our own efforts.

Nevertheless, many people are convinced that money will fulfill their emotional needs. As they treat themselves to everything money can buy, they do not understand why their lives are so empty, why they are so full of anxieties, why they are so lonely and so lost. They spend more and more to correct the situation, but the more they spend the more miserable they become. And the less money they have.

The way we do or do not spend money follows the same continuum as other behaviors. Most of us are inside the bell curve which represents the norm. No matter how rich or poor we are, we live more or less within our incomes.

But at the extremes on either side of the bell curve, life is far from this normalcy. At one end, there are people who lead constipated lives dedicated to amassing and saving money. Multimillionaires have been known to live like paupers. At the other extreme are those who spend way beyond their means in a fruitless search for emotional comfort and often find themselves both financially and emotionally bankrupt. People like Hannah.

## THE IMPULSIVE/COMPULSIVE SHOPPER

From time to time, Hannah would spend as if there were no tomorrow. She had a closet full of clothes she had never worn and a desk full of bills that kept her awake nights. "No one would ever believe the extent of my wardrobe," she said. "Or my bills. I wear the same three or four outfits to the office day after day. I brown-bag it at lunch. I walk to work unless it is pouring buckets. I spent my last vacation behind the counter at McDonald's flipping hamburgers, so I could pay the interest on my credit-card balances.

"I know it's crazy, but I just can't help it. Every so often, I go mad at the mall or I'll go into New York and spend my way up and down Madison Avenue. I'll buy everything that appeals to me, things that I'll never have the occasion to wear. Last Saturday, I bought an evening gown on sale for $900 marked down from $1,200—and I already have two evening dresses that I've never worn. And then I dropped $500 on cosmetics and lotions. I felt great.

"But the next morning I felt sick. I could not believe I had spent all that money for a dress I didn't need or want now that I had it. I couldn't return it, because it was a sale item. So here I am with another enormous charge on my credit card. One of these days I'm going to get in trouble."

Hannah was already in trouble, whether she realized it or not. She had huge balances on all seven of her credit cards. The interest payments barely left enough to pay her basic living expenses. There came the month when she could not pay the rent. She had less than $50 in her checking account. It was three weeks until her next paycheck.

She asked her boss for an advance, saying that she had had some unexpected expenses. "You don't have anything put aside for emergencies?" he asked. She ended up telling him the truth.

"You've got a problem," he said. "You better take care of it before it's too late." He had attended a seminar where I had discussed self-defeating behaviors in business and professional life. I had given each participant his own Psychological Tool Kit—a box of cards describing each psychological technique and giving examples of situations in which they could be used. He told Hannah about the seminar and gave her his Psychological Tool Kit. "You might try this approach," he said. "It made a lot of sense to me."

As she was leaving his office, he called her back. "You know," he told her, "no one can do a good job when their finances are all out of kilter." She got the message.

That night, she emptied her clothes closets and tried everything on. Several of the outfits she had never worn were good-looking. She would start wearing them to work. She packed up the rest to take to a consignment shop that sold high-quality, almost-new clothes. Then she cut up her credit cards.

That weekend she studied the cards in the Psychological Tool Kit and decided that the first thing she had to do was find out why she was driven to these shopping binges. This meant working on a Basic Diagnostic List. Her first list read like this:

| Best Qualities | Worst Qualities | Goals |
|---|---|---|
| Tops at my job | Worrying | Get out of debt |
| Reliable | Spree-shopping | Stop the stress |
| Imaginative | No self-control | Have more fun |

Her next step was to work out a budget. She drew up a spending plan designed to pay off her credit-card debt in a year. To help herself stick to it, she recorded everything she spent in a small notebook, totaling it every night. This was a financial version of the Reinforcement List. When she was under budget, she would add a positive note to the week's entries, something like, "I'm in control of myself and my money, and I'm doing splendidly." When she overspent, she would make a note of the reason. Then she would add something reassuring such as, "I went off the track this week, but not too badly. I'll try to do better next time. I know I can." The combination of writing down what she spent and giving herself as much Positive Reinforcement as she could kept her budget goal in the forefront of her consciousness and made it easier to watch her spending.

The notebook also acted as a conscience. One Saturday afternoon, she could not resist the impulse to go shopping. She bought two sweaters in one shop and a pair of gloves in another, paying by check. She was trying on a blazer in a third store when she thought of the notebook. She was horrified. "I can't do this!" she told herself.

She took off the blazer, went back to the other stores, returned her purchases and fled. It was the first time she had ever broken off a shopping spree in midstream. She felt immensely pleased with herself when she got home—and a bit shaky as she realized how near she had been to a binge.

She had to find a way to curb these sudden impulses to splurge. She found the answer in the Psychological Tool Kit: Negative Reinforcement. She used the same technique that Rhonda had used to cut down on her nagging—the rubber-band bracelet. She added another deterrent that she dreamed up herself. Whenever she had an irresistible impulse to go shopping, she went to the movies instead. This was an excellent idea. It not only kept her out of the stores, it substituted something pleasurable for a self-defeating behavior.

## JUST ONE STEP

We all do things on impulse. Sometimes these impulses seem irresistible. A hungry mouse gave behavioral scientists a valuable insight into human impulsiveness. The mouse was placed at the bottom of the stem of a T-shaped maze. Food had been placed at the extreme ends of the stroke across the top of the T.

The mouse, smelling the food, scampered down the long corridor of the T and then started scooting back and forth between the arms of the T. It never got as far as the food. It would run a few inches to the right and then go back and run a few inches to the left. It ran back and forth, back and forth, seemingly crazed because it could not decide which way to go. Finally, in experiment after experiment, the mouse took just one extra step to the right or the left—and that determined the direction in which it finally ran to get the food. Just that one extra uncalculated step was enough to determine which way it would go.

People are much the same. Our impulsive behavior is usually dictated by just one step. Physiologist Benjamin Libet discovered that the unconscious initiates the impulse to action, and the conscious then okays or vetoes it. Professor Libet's experiments showed that the conscious did not kick in until about half a second after the impulse was formed. While this is a mere eye-blink of time, it is long enough to take that first step before the conscious even knows what is going on in the unconscious.

This is why an immediate negative response to Hannah's impulses to go shopping was so effective. The minute the thought entered her mind, she snapped that rubber band. Her conscious was alerted before she could give in to the impulse. Then she took herself to the movies where she escaped into another world for two hours and left her anxieties and loneliness behind.

I want to point out that there is nothing wrong in buying a sweater or a pair of gloves or anything else on impulse. In fact, studies show that women who occasionally buy on impulse are psychologically happier and healthier. It gives them a lift and makes them feel good about themselves. But these women's impulses are simply that—impulses. They are not driven to buy. The sweater is not a substitute for love. The gloves are not a desperate effort to keep loneliness at bay. They simply see something they like and treat themselves every now and then. They are in the realm of the golden mean when it comes to spending behavior.

As Hannah worked on her Basic Diagnostic List from week to week, she spent a lot of time trying to analyze her shopping sprees. They seemed so out-of-character. At work, she was controlled, competent and in complete charge of what she was doing. She used her old credit-card statements to track her impulsive, compulsive buying binges and found a common denominator.

## TACKLING THE REAL PROBLEM

Her shopping forays were confined to weekends, usually when she was feeling lonely and full of vague anxieties. Her spending was like a feel-good pill. The more she bought, the better she felt—until the morning after.

When she had reached this point in her analysis, it was easy to put two and two together. The buying binges were an attempt to make up for the missing elements in her life. Shopping was the quick fix that provided a certain companionship with the sales people in the stores and made her feel like someone who counted, someone worthwhile, someone who spent money on expensive clothes and accessories.

At the end of the month, Hannah made out the last of the Basic Diagnostic Lists, the Master List. It read:

| Best Qualities | Worst Qualities | Goals |
|---|---|---|
| Decisive | Unable to control buying | Pay debts |
| Imaginative | Self-doubting | Stop buying |
| Self-starter | Anxiety | Make friends |

She had learned a lot about herself in those four weeks. Her assessments of her best and worst qualities had sharpened and her goals, while essentially the same, had been clarified. Now, analyzing her best and worst qualities, she found interesting contradictions.

She was decisive, yet could not control her impulsive, compulsive spending. She was a self-starter, which implied a certain amount of self-confidence, yet she was full of self-doubt and anxiety.

"It seems as if I have a double life," she wrote in her diary. "My best qualities predominate at work. My worst govern the rest of my life. I don't seem to know how to talk to people about anything except business. As a result, most weekends I don't talk to anybody. There are times when I would give anything to have someone I could call on the spur of the moment and say, 'How about a movie? . . . Do you feel like going for a walk? . . . Are you in the mood for pizza?' But I don't have any friends like that. If I call one of my neighbors, they'll be surprised because I don't really know them, and they'll probably be busy anyway. There are times when I feel terribly alone in the world," she concluded.

As she studied her Diagnostic Lists and thought about the changes she had made in her life in the past month, she understood that there was no way she could conquer the impulse to buy, unless she conquered her loneliness. Her lack of self-esteem inhibited her from reaching out to people. And until she could do that, she would not be able to shake the loneliness that drove her out of the house and off to the mall. There were no miracles, no magic. If she wanted her life to change, she would have to change it herself.

She went back to the Psychological Tool Kit. It suggested using the Rehearsal Techniques for shyness, loneliness, lack of self-confidence, for preparing oneself for a new lifestyle. It was a thumbnail self-portrait.

She would Act As If she were not lonely by surrounding herself with people. As a start, she asked a coworker and her husband and a couple who lived in the same apartment building for dinner one Saturday.

She Previsualized the whole thing, from cleaning the apartment to the food and wine she would serve and the topics she would introduce if the conversation flagged. At seven o'clock that Saturday evening, she began Acting As If. She Acted As If she had people to dinner all the time, as if she felt confident that the evening would be pleasant and that everyone would enjoy themselves.

It worked. They chatted about movies they had seen, discussed the pros and cons of having a car in the city and why it was that men's haircuts cost so much less than women's. When her guests left, Hannah felt triumphant. She had done it. It had gone well. And she had enjoyed it.

A few weeks later, she invited the same group and a few other people from work to watch the Sunday morning talk shows and then have brunch. When they left, they told her how stimulating it had been. Little by little, she reached out to people and soon she found herself being included in their weekend activities. Now that she had taken the first steps, the Ripple Effect was working for her.

A year later, Hannah was out of debt. She no longer uses shopping as a quick fix for her self-esteem or an escape from loneliness, because now she has friends. And her self-image today is of a strong woman who was able to overcome a self-defeating trait and put her life on a positive track.

## ASSOCIATED TRAITS

Impulse spending is not the only self-defeating trait associated with low self-esteem that stems from the belief that money is the key to happiness. Other related traits include such behaviors as spending a disproportionate part of one's income on rent in order to have a fashionable address, even though this means the furnishings are limited to a bed, a table and a chair. There are people who will spend a fortune on a foreign sports car or a boat, even if it means they have to live at poverty level.

It may be that the fashionable address or the elegant sports car fills a real desire. It may be something you really want even though, given your salary, it is fantastically impractical. You may accept the trade-off of denying yourself in other areas. If so, fine. Everyone is entitled to spend their incomes as they please. But this is rarely the case. More often it is a desire to enhance one's image and thus increase one's self-esteem.

People who spend inordinately for what amounts to a facade or stage setting usually want to be accepted as someone who leads the life that the penthouse or the sports car seems to reflect. A kind of magical thinking often goes along with this behavior. It is as if once they have one of the symbols of the kind of life they idealize, somehow the lifestyle will be achieved, and people will regard them more highly. It is an expensive attempt at bolstering their self-image, and one that never works.

The first step in controlling such spending is to recognize, as Hannah did, that your behavior is self-defeating, and to try to find out what is causing it with the aid of the Basic Diagnostic List. The second step is to fill the real need in your life. You cannot order up love like a pizza, or banish loneliness with a flick of a remote control. You have to reach out. You have to give love as well as receive it. You cannot acquire status and success simply by buying its symbols. You have to earn them. But you can work to boost your self-image so that you no longer are the victim of false values and false beliefs.

*Chapter Thirteen*

# Boasting

---

## Putting Your Worst Foot Forward

---

DON'T YOU GET fed up with the woman who tells you her husband never forgets an anniversary, and the grandmother who claims her ten-year-old darling gets all A's and was voted most popular fifth-grader, and your colleague who can't stop talking about her ability to pick stocks and how well her portfolio is doing?

Sometimes such constant boasting is hard to take, but you should feel sorry for the people who do it. They have a great big empty hole where their self-esteem should be. They are convinced that they just don't measure up. And boasting is the way they try to compensate for their self-esteem deficit.

Boasters are trying to convince you that they are brighter, richer, happier, kinder, wittier, more successful, more lovable than they think they are. Unfortunately, it does not work. Instead of convincing you that they are bright, witty, rich and lovable, you perceive them as obnoxious, pretentious and unlikable. And they definitely do not improve their self-image. Otherwise they would stop boasting!

*Example:* The woman who brags about the great deal she negotiated on her new house. "I got it for $20,000 under the asking price," she claims. "The Realtor couldn't believe they would take my offer. He said he wished he had my smarts." You happen to know that the seller was delighted with the price she got. It was more than she had expected.

*Message:* You should respect me because I'm an unbelievably shrewd businesswoman and an expert negotiator. I want you to be impressed with me.

*Example:* At the PTA meeting, you compliment a woman you barely know on her suit. "It's a Chanel," she tells you. "It cost an arm and a leg, but," she shrugs, "what can you do?" You are wearing your trusty blazer and a no-name skirt, and you tell yourself it will be a cold day in hell before you compliment her again.

*Message:* I am someone special. I can afford to spend whatever I want on whatever I want. I want you to admire me.

Each woman was trying to bolster her self-image by boasting, but failed. Each made an unfavorable impression—one as a liar, the other as an insensitive show-off. Boasting is a very close relative of lying. The dividing line between the two is sometimes almost invisible. But the causes are different. Boasters have a self-esteem deficit and are trying to bolster it. Liars, as I explain in the next chapter, are either looking for an easy way out—an excuse—or are trying to take advantage of you in one way or another.

Boasters are as transparent as a windowpane. Those who boast about money wish they had as much as they try to make you believe they do. People who boast about their sex life tend to be covering up their feeling that it should be better, that something is missing. Those who boast about their famous and influential friends wish that they themselves were famous and influential. People who boast about their clothes or homes or automobiles are starved for admiration, appreciation, anything that will make them feel as good as the next person. Boasting is usually fairly innocent, but always self-defeating, because it accomplishes the exact opposite of what the boaster wants and needs.

## ARE YOU A BOASTER?

Incredible as it seems, most boasters are not aware of what they are doing and even more blissfully unaware of the negative effect it has on people. They may realize that for some reason people do not seem to cotton to them and that they never succeed in getting close to other people. But they have no idea that it is their boasting that is blocking them from the acceptance they crave. They believe it is because they are not famous or rich or bright enough.

How do you find out whether or not boasting is the problem in your relationships? The ideal way would be to carry a tape recorder around for a few days and then play back your conversations. If you are constantly pointing out how great you are, that your new car is at the top of the automotive hit parade, that your daughter is a genius, then boasting is a problem and you would do well to bring this behavior closer to the norm. But taping conversations is impractical and may get you into trouble. Since most people are completely oblivious of their boasting, the Basic Diagnostic List is only minimally helpful. I have yet to see a Basic Diagnostic List in which anyone cited boasting as a worst quality. The Diagnostic List, however, will pinpoint traits that reveal a lack of self-esteem. If it does, then you should ask yourself if you are trying to compensate for your poor self-image by boasting. Educate your ear to pick up on your boasting. When you catch yourself at it, classify its degree of offensiveness. Boasting ranges from bad to worse.

Bad is telling your coworkers that the boss said you were the only one he could count on in a crunch. This kind of boasting is stupid as well as self-defeating. It turns off the people you work with and it will undoubtedly get back to the boss, who will realize what poor judgment you have and what a blabbermouth you are.

Worse is when you combine a boast with a put-down. For instance, when you tell the happy owner of a mutt that you have always had purebred dogs. "You have to pay for the bloodline, but then you have a dog worth having." Or when your sister-in-law telephones excitedly to say that they have enough Frequent Flyer miles for two economy round-trips to Paris, and you say, "Jim and I always go business class. It's so much more comfortable."

This kind of put-down boasting alienates more people than bad breath or mother-in-law jokes. And faster. Your newly sensitized ear should be able to detect either type of boasting. If it does, make a double check. Sometimes we judge ourselves too severely. Go to the source. Ask yourself, "Do I boast?" Don't answer right away. Let the idea percolate in your head for three or four days.

Julie began listening to herself with an ear tuned to boasting. When she realized that she did exaggerate from time to time, she asked herself, "Do I boast?" And on the morning of the fourth day, she had looked at herself in the mirror as she was brushing her teeth and said, "Yes, I do. I boast a lot. I think I made a fool of myself yesterday."

She had monopolized the conversation at the garden club meeting. She had started talking about how her secret composting formula had produced tomatoes and asparagus that were the envy of her neighbors. And her strawberries had been so large and red and sweet that the man next door had begged for her formula. It was all brag. Julie had no secret formula. She simply followed standard composting procedures. Her strawberries and all the rest had done well, but no better than anyone else's.

When the conversation veered to clothes, she had taken over again. "I've just got to tell you this. Last week I was walking down Michigan Avenue and a woman stopped me. She wanted to know if I was a model. When I shook my head, she said, "Well, you should be, the way you wear clothes.'" Actually, the woman had stopped her to ask where she could get a bus. She had thanked Julie for the directions and said, "That's a very pretty scarf you are wearing."

Driving home with Katherine after the meeting, Julie had started talking about her hairdresser. "He's the best in Chicago," she had said. Katherine had gone sort of "uh-huh" and started talking about the program for the next garden club meeting.

## TOOLS FOR CHANGE

Julie took the first step toward change by admitting to herself that she boasted and that her boasting was not doing her any good. Just being aware of a self-defeating trait tends to curb it. But Julie, like almost all serious boasters, needed more than awareness.

She started with a double-barreled dose of Negative Reinforcement. The rubber-band bracelet was too conspicuous. She did not want to have to explain what she was doing. She settled for a hard pinch on her forearm whenever she caught herself boasting.

At the same time, she tried to turn her boast into a compliment if at all possible. When Julie caught herself referring to her "prizewinning meatloaf," she gave herself an unobtrusive hard pinch and immediately said, "Actually I'm exaggerating. But I hope I'll hit on a prizewinning recipe someday. I know you're a terrific cook. I bought the coffee cake you made for the garden club fund-raiser. My husband raved about it." You have to be a quick thinker to make this kind of switch, but compliments— real ones—make more friends than boasts.

Julie also started two lists—a Negative and a Positive Reinforcement List. Each time she caught herself bragging, she made a note in the Negative Reinforcement List of what she said and why she said it.

The why was sometimes hard to pinpoint. "Why did I tell Patrick that I speak French fluently when I only know a few phrases? Why did I make a point of letting Meg know how much

I paid for those Ferragamo shoes? Why did I tell those people that my sister was a friend of the President's wife when all she did was shake her hand in a reception line?" It is hard to admit to yourself that you will say almost anything to impress people. But most of her boasting was an effort to impress others, and quite often it was an attempt to show that she was superior to them in some way.

The Positive Reinforcement List was simply an itemizing of her good traits and her accomplishments. She spent a few minutes on it once a week, adding to it as she thought of new positive characteristics and achievements.

At the end of the month, she went over both lists. The Negative Reinforcement List showed that her bragging had gone way down. There was a significant change.

The Positive Reinforcement List had more entries than she had thought possible. She had not realized that she had so many accomplishments and positive characteristics. It made her feel a lot better about herself. She realized that she did not have to exaggerate and boast to convince people that she was a really special and worthwhile person. All she had to do was give them a chance to find out for themselves.

She continued both lists for another month. By then she had cut her boasting down to an absolute minimum. Her arm was no longer full of little black-and-blue spots from being pinched. Since it takes at least six to eight weeks to establish a new behavior, Julie decided to continue her Negative Reinforcement List for another month just to make sure that her new behavior was well established.

## THE PERMISSIBLE BOAST

There is nothing wrong with giving yourself a pat on the back every now and then or in sharing your delight in a piece of good news or good fortune. Just be sensitive about the time and the place, and beware of overkill. The truth is that only a handful of people are going to be really happy for you. The typical reaction to someone else's good fortune—deserved or undeserved—is often envy.

If your daughter's SAT scores were the highest in her class, go ahead, boast about it. Let your family and close friends know how proud and delighted you are. Just be careful not to boast in front of the other parents whose youngsters' scores were lower.

If you got a fat raise, you certainly deserve to boast about it. But not at the office. And certainly not in front of Grace, whose husband just got fired after twenty years with the company. Keep it for your nearest and dearest.

Boasting can never establish a positive Halo Effect. Quite the opposite. People regard boasters as insufferable. But once you tame the urge and bring your boasting closer to the norm, there are times when it can be effective, a positive rather than a negative quality.

For instance, "I have the best friends in the world—loyal, lovable and Einstein-bright," and "This garden club is head and shoulders above any other garden club in the state. And I know. I'm a member" are effective, positive boasts. Why? Because you are saluting the group, establishing your kinship with them, extolling their virtues and only incidentally patting yourself on the back for having such great friends or belonging to such a great club. These boasts will not turn anyone off—not even members of another garden club. They may think your club is full of weeds and nerds, but they will appreciate your loyalty.

# Chapter Fourteen

# LYING AND GULLIBILITY

## The Good, The Bad and The Ugly
## Behind These Traits

FROM THE TIME we could toddle, we were warned against lying. George Washington became a child's storybook hero because he " 'fessed up to felling the cherry tree." Pinocchio's nose grew longer every time he told a whopper. Honesty, we were told, is by far the best policy.

Yet studies reveal that 90 percent of us admit we tell lies (and the other 10 percent are probably lying). We lie about everything from our age to our dress size. Seventy percent of husbands and wives admit that they lie to each other. And 75 percent of us lie to our friends. Shocking? Not really.

Most lies are kindly, even loving. As novelist Graham Greene wrote, ". . . kindness and lies are worth a thousand truths." Kind lies, known as white lies, are the common, garden-variety fibs that ease our relationships with others. Women tell most of them. When he asks, "How was it for you?" are you going to say, "I wish we'd watched David Letterman"? Of course not. The answer, as all women know, is, "It was wonderful, darling."

When your sister-in-law shows up at Thanksgiving in a ghastly new outfit and asks you how you like it, you tell her, "You look as if you stepped right out of the pages of *Vogue*" or

"I love that color on you." Who wants to ruin a family get-together with the brutal truth?

We tell such lies not only to protect other people's feelings, but also to protect ourselves. I don't know how often I've asked my secretary to tell callers that I am not there when I am in the next room concentrating on writing my column or preparing a lecture. I feel it might hurt them if she said I was too busy to take their call at that moment.

We tell alibi lies to get ourselves off the hook, to cover up our mistakes or our thoughtlessness. You are twenty minutes late for your lunch date, because you stopped to look at sweaters that were on sale. You rush into the restaurant and tell your friend. "I thought I'd never get here. There was an accident and traffic was backed up for miles." This seems harmless, but could eventually be self-defeating. This kind of lie reveals a disregard for your friend's time and feelings that may lose you her friendship if you make a habit of it.

Some alibi lies come home to roost with disastrous consequences, as Janine discovered. Her boss asked her to make hotel and plane reservations for his trip to Los Angeles and arrange for a car and driver to meet him at the airport. When she gave him his tickets, he said, "I better have the telephone number for the car service, just in case."

Janine swallowed hard. She had completely forgotten to arrange for the car and driver. "I'm sorry," she alibied. "You will have to take a taxi. The car services are all out on strike."

In Los Angeles, her boss mentioned the strike to a colleague. "Strike? There's no strike," he was told. He fired Janine by telephone. Alibi lies can boomerang and, like Janine, the liar becomes the victim of her own lie.

Then there are the truly hateful lies, the malicious, malevolent and manipulative lies, all of which are cruel and harmful. Evelyn tells Sara that "Louise says you are the most boring woman she knows. I'm just telling you this for your own good. I know you like her, but she's no friend of yours."

Why would someone be this hateful? Usually out of fear or

jealousy or insecurity or all three. Evelyn, insecure, fears that Sara likes Louise better than she likes her. Her malicious lie gives Evelyn a momentary sense of power, but her lie will probably boomerang.

Once Sara stops to think, she will realize that Louise does not think her boring at all. Quite the contrary. Evelyn will have accomplished the very thing she wanted to avert. She will have destroyed her friendship with Sara.

Some cruel lies are told by very decent people who become confused by conflicting priorities or loyalties. Maria and Philip were planning to buy a house. Maria was worried. There were rumors that her company might merge with another.

She decided to talk to her boss. "We've found a house we want to buy," she said, "but I'm concerned about these merger rumors. Would a merger affect my job? We won't be able to swing the mortgage payments without my salary."

"Not to worry," the boss assured her. "I can't comment on the rumors, but you don't need to worry about your job."

The week after Maria and Philip closed on their new house, the merger was announced. Maria and several others were given their walking papers.

It is understandable that her boss could not comment on the merger, but his lie was unnecessary and cruel. He could easily have said something like, "Who knows what will happen?" without disclosing any privileged information. This might have saved Maria and her husband from financial disaster.


## WHY WE BELIEVE LIES

If something sounds too good to be true, it probably is. Your inner alarm should start buzzing, but nine times out of ten, you believe what you are being told. When you look back, you realize you should have known better. Why were you so self-destructively gullible?

Manipulative liars twist the truth because they want something. An unethical stockbroker might tell a client that he is putting every penny he can scrape together into Dotty Devices. "Their stock is going to triple in the next six months. They're about to market an automatic shoelace. Orders are pouring in already."

"Wonderful!" the client exclaims. "That's just the kind of investment I'm looking for."

Well, the only place Dotty Devices and its automatic shoelace is going is down the drain. The only one to profit will be the broker whose commission is already in his pocket. The gullible buyer will have lost his money. He should have been more careful, you say, insisted on more information about the proposed investment.

The investor's problem was that he wanted to believe the broker. Most victims want to believe the lies they are told—and liars know it. Psychiatrist Paul Ekman of the University of California at San Francisco, who has been studying liars for twenty years, says that willing victims are the major reason liars are successful. Probably the most disastrous of such liar-victim collaborations occurred in 1938 when Prime Minister Neville Chamberlain of Great Britain believed Hitler's lie that he would not invade Czechoslovakia despite the signs that war was inevitable. If Chamberlain had not bought Hitler's lie, it would have meant that all his years of appeasing the dictator had been in vain. He *needed* to believe that he had done the right thing as a statesman, that his policy toward Hitler had been correct.


## HOW TO TELL WHEN SOMEONE IS LYING

There is nothing more self-defeating than believing a liar, especially a malevolent or manipulative liar. We do not need to swallow their lies hook, line and sinker, no matter how alluring they may be.

It is not easy to tell when someone is lying to you, but there are clues. Dr. Ekman says that in all his years of studying lies and liars, he has found no foolproof way of detecting a lie. Liars are usually good actors. They look you straight in the eye, speak clearly and convincingly. They radiate sincerity.

Dr. Ekman says that inexperienced liars often give themselves away by hesitating before answering a question that should elicit an immediate response, such as, "Where were you last night?" or "Who did you have lunch with today?" or by constantly looking away while talking.

The professional liar, who may be a con man or a politician, a salesman or a diplomat, avoids such behaviors, but often gives himself away by moving his hands to his face. A gesture toward the nose, researchers say, can be a giveaway. The tension between what the brain knows and what the diplomat is saying causes small physiological changes that affect the sensitive nasal membranes. They itch and the hand moves toward the nose.

And there is one telltale trait, Dr. Ekman says, that most liars cannot control. This is rapid eye blinking, a sure sign of nervousness (or an eye irritation). The next time someone tries to sell you the Brooklyn Bridge, watch his eyes. He will probably be blinking.

The best way to keep from being the victim of a manipulative liar is to cultivate skepticism. You do not need to become a misanthrope or a pessimist believing everyone is out to get you. All you want to do is move your belief in the goodness of your fellow man into the realm of reality.

The following three questions will help you sharpen your skepticism and provide an antidote to gullibility. If the unfortunate investor in Dotty Devices had asked himself these questions, he would have been better off.

1. Why is he telling me this?

Why was that stockbroker who was peddling Dotty Devices willing to let you in on the ground floor? After all, this is the first time you have met with this broker. He must have regular clients who would have snapped up the stock already if it were as good as he said it was.

### 2. Why should I believe him?

The broker will make a commission if he sells you a block of stock, but unless he gives you copies of past annual reports and financial statements, research on the company, its officers and its other products, you have no reason to believe him, no matter how convincing and enthusiastic he is. If he gives you the information you want, take it home and study it. If the stock is a good buy today, it will be a good buy next week.

### 3. Why do I believe him?

The truthful answer may be that you believe his sales pitch because you want to make a killing in the stock market. You like the idea of tripling your money in six months. You are willing to suspend disbelief because the bait is so alluring.

These questions can be applied to almost any situation where people are telling you what you want to hear.

When your son tells you he is not on drugs, you accept this— even though he has been exhibiting all the classic symptoms of drug use that were in the flyer his school sent to parents. You want to believe him, because the truth is too unpleasant.

When your daughter tells you that the reason she did not get home until five o'clock Saturday morning was because her boyfriend's car broke down, you believe her. You don't ask why she didn't telephone so you could come get them. You really don't want to think about what she was doing. You are a willing victim of her lie.

When your husband tells you week after week, four nights out of five, that he won't be home until late, that the boss has asked him to do this or that, you believe him. You do not want to face the possibility of infidelity.

Thoughtful, honest answers to these three questions will help you move yourself along the continuum from acquiescent gullibility to the norm of healthy suspicion. It may make you uncomfortable at first, because you really don't want the truth. But without the truth, you are not going to be able to help your son or daughter—or yourself.

## HOW CAN A LIAR CHANGE HIS SPOTS?

Habitual kindly liars and alibi liars can nudge this basically useless behavior closer to the norm fairly easily, if they want to. And they should, because eventually their lies will diminish the quality of their lives.

The kindly lie does not hurt anyone—except, occasionally, the liar. The kindly lie often makes someone feel good about herself and very rarely backfires. It becomes self-defeating, however, when overdone. If you habitually tell people they look wonderful even though they have a cold and their nose is red and their hair is a mess, people will consider you insincere and find your well-meant lies irritating. They will wonder why you are so anxious to ingratiate yourself.

Alibi lies can boomerang as others realize that you always have an unavoidable "emergency." If you are an habitual alibi-liar, you will eventually lose your credibility and your friends. The habitual alibi-liar almost inevitably gets caught in a web of deceit—and whether the lies are harmless or not, no one feels quite the same about her again.

Lies like Janine's are both stupid and self-defeating. She lost her job because she lied about a careless mistake. If she had told the truth about forgetting to arrange for a car and driver, she could have arranged for the car while he was in transit. Her boss would have been annoyed, but it is unlikely that he would have fired her. His chagrin at talking about a nonexistent strike to his business contacts made him far angrier than he would have been if she had told the truth.

The easiest way to cut down on kindly lies and alibi lies is to use a Negative Reinforcement List. Get a little notebook you can put in your pocket or handbag and every time you tell a lie, make a note of it. What you said and why.

Once a week, go over your list and analyze your lies. Why did you lie? Because you were late? Because you forgot? Because you did not want to do whatever it was? These are the behaviors you want to change. Once you change them, you will have no need to lie.

If you are always late and always making up excuses about it, resolve to start fifteen minutes earlier.

If you forgot whatever it was you were supposed to do, resolve to make a to-do list on your desk calendar or pocket diary. And don't forget to check your diary every morning.

If you lied because it was something you did not want to do, you should not have committed to it, and your problem may be an inability to say no. In this case, write out a Worst-Case Scenario. If you are asked to do something you do not want to do, figure out the worst that could happen if you said no. If the worst would be really bad, then say yes—and make sure you follow through on whatever it is.

There are times, of course, when you won't have the opportunity to make out a Scenario. In these cases, think fast. Remind yourself that if you say Yes, you must do it and not let yourself make a lying excuse. If you really do not want to do it and do not have to do it, say no. Your life will be much simpler, and you will be much more popular.

Continue the list for six weeks. This is the minimum time it takes to establish a new behavior. You should find that you are making fewer fictional excuses as the weeks go by. Just being conscious of what you are doing helps you cut down, and changing the behavior that triggered the lies helps even more.

If you are still a bit shaky at the end of six weeks, keep up the list for another three weeks just to be sure the nonlying behavior is firmly established.

As you get used to telling the truth ("I'm sorry I'm late. I just didn't leave early enough" or "I just plain forgot to put the income tax in the mail" or "It was my fault. I was not paying attention and didn't see the stop sign"), you realize that telling the truth is easier than dreaming up alibis.

There may be times when you feel a kindly, white lie is necessary. If so, tell it. But don't let yourself slip back into the habit of trying to cover up mistakes, omissions, lateness and forgetfulness with alibi lies. In the long run, it is far simpler to change your behavior.

Unfortunately, malevolent and manipulative lies are not as easily controlled. There is as little likelihood that malevolent or manipulative liars will want to change as there is that the leopard will change his spots, but the rare soul who does want to stop this lying should seek professional help.

The psychological tools I offer in this book are not enough to straighten out these liars' hostility, fears, jealousies and insecurities. This kind of lying is not susceptible to do-it-yourself therapy. It takes time and hard work on the part of both patient and therapist to root out the causes of habitual cruel lying, but the rewards are immeasurable.

# Chapter Fifteen

# JEALOUSY

---

## Getting Control of the Seventh Sin

---

JEALOUSY MAY BE the loneliest emotion in the world, even lonelier than grief. The grieving woman has friends and relatives who share her sorrow, but the jealous woman stands by herself. A thousand fears besiege her, all revolving around abandonment and loss and helplessness. Her emotions bewilder and dizzy her, and she feels so vulnerable it is as if her very skin is raw. Even the strongest self-esteem is weakened by jealousy.

I will never forget a scene my husband and I witnessed in a fashionable New York restaurant one night some ten years ago. Two very well-dressed and attractive couples were at a table near us. Both men were completely involved with one of the women. They leaned toward her, smiled at her, flirted with her. They ignored the second woman, despite her efforts to join in the conversation. Each time she tried, her husband would glance at her, say something and turn back to the other woman.

It was obvious that she was more than uncomfortable. She was jealous of the attention being paid to the other woman while she was ignored. And hurt. I could almost see the anger building up. Her whole body stiffened. Her lips tightened. I wondered what would happen. She was obviously too much of a lady to make a scene in public.

A few minutes later, she got up, smiled at her companions and left. It was at least half an hour before the others realized she had been gone a long time. The other woman was dispatched to the ladies' room to check on her. She returned, shaking her head. The headwaiter was summoned. There was a short conversation. Her husband asked for the check and the three left immediately.

I asked our waiter what had happened. "She left," he told us. "She asked us to call her a taxi."

I thought she had handled the situation beautifully. Without making a scene, she got the message across that she was not going to stand for being ignored and humiliated. I have always wondered what happened when her husband came home.

Was she in bed pretending to be asleep? Was she curled up on the living-room sofa crying her eyes out? Was she waiting at the door—fury in her eyes and acid in her words? Was she in the living room by the fire—passed-out drunk? Was she on the telephone telling her best friend what bastards her husband and his friend were? And what a slut the other woman was? Did she throw something at him? Or was she waiting, perfectly composed, to discuss her feelings about the evening?

What would you have done? Think about it. You will learn something about yourself.

Any of these reactions, except the last and possibly the first, would be counterproductive, although perfectly normal and understandable. A woman may feel better for having let off emotional steam, but she loses control of the situation. I explain why a few pages later on.

There may be a woman here and there who has never experienced this emotion, but not many. In a survey of some 750 people, 54 percent described themselves as jealous. The other 46 percent said they were not jealous at the time, although they had experienced jealousy previously. Another survey found that 96 percent of the participants had been jealous. One-third of the couples seeking help for troubled marriages have jealousy problems.

Chances are that you are a normally jealous woman. If you take that bell curve formed by Reversion to the Mean, 95 percent of jealousy falls within the curve, within the realm of normalcy. On either side of the curve, 2.5 percent of the population is either abnormally lacking in jealousy or so jealous that they can be described as neurotic. A woman in the latter category, a woman who falls prey to jealousy every time her husband looks at another woman, should seek professional help to prevent this out-of-control jealousy from destroying her life. But for the rest of us, jealousy is an absolutely normal, although agonizing, emotion and coping with it can be a do-it-yourself project.

## THE THREE CARDINAL RULES FOR DEALING WITH JEALOUSY

I will never know what happened with the woman who left the restaurant, but I do know what happened in a real-life episode of jealousy.

Shari was almost literally green with jealousy, so jealous that her stomach was upset. Her husband, Irving, was having an affair with a coworker, Donna. She had seen them herself. She had been shopping and decided to have tea at The Plaza before she went home. As she entered the Palm Court, she saw them at a table, absolutely wrapped up in each other.

She turned on her heel and left. All day, she told herself, "I bet he'll be late. I'll bet he calls to say he has to work late." And sure enough, Irving called. "I have to work late," he said, "but I should be home around eight."

The evening was tense. Irving could not figure out why Shari was in such a state. She kept making pointed remarks about men who led double lives. Finally she burst out, "You can stop lying. I saw you with Donna at The Plaza! Is that what you call working late?"

He stared at her. "Is that what this is all about? Donna and I were waiting for that new client I was telling you about, the one who wants to switch his business to us. I brought Donna along because she worked up our proposal. And why the hell are you spying on me?" He had worked himself into a state of angry indignation.

Shari was humiliated. Irving was obviously telling the truth, and she had made a fool of herself. Jealousy has a way of making people do that. As far as the dynamics of the marriage were concerned, Shari had lost power. She had shown herself to be the vulnerable partner, more dependent on him than he was on her.

Jealousy is self-defeating. The jealous woman lives in fear of loss: loss of love, loss of a way of life, loss of status. To be jealous is to have a shaky self-image.

Shari's marriage had never been in danger, but it was never quite the same again and neither was her self-esteem. She could have handled the situation more intelligently.

If you are jealous, it is important to examine the reasons for your jealousy before saying, hinting or doing anything. If the reasons are valid and rational, you do something about the situation. If they are irrational, based on fear, insecurity and an overactive imagination, you do something about yourself.

If Shari had known the three cardinal rules for dealing with jealousy, she would have handled the situation better. These rules are:

1. *Get yourself under control before doing or saying anything. No matter how upset you are, Act As If you were calm and life is on an even keel.*

Go for a walk. Play a few sets of tennis. Go bike riding with the children. Mow the lawn. Clean house. Exercise stimulates endorphin production, those brain chemicals that make you feel better. While you are working off your jealous turmoil, keep telling yourself that you are in control. You are going to Act As If you are not jealous, no matter what.

2. *Avoid any confrontation until you are at least 90 percent sure you have reason to be jealous. Do some serious thinking about why you are jealous and whether or not your jealousy is rational or irrational.*

Here are four typical jealous-wife situations. Choose the one that most resembles your own. It may take a stretch of the imagination, but one of them should be fairly close.

SITUATION: I am jealous because he paid so much attention to that blonde at the cocktail party and none to me. It's the same at every affair we go to. He is always more interested in other women than in me.

ANALYSIS: A party is a party. You are expected to circulate. Your husband was simply being a good guest. I hope you also took the opportunity to meet new people. The more people each of you meet, the more fun you will have hashing it over later. Perhaps you feel more dependent on the relationship than he does. If so, hanging on his arm is not going to make you feel any better. You may want to consider pumping up your self-image and becoming a more equal partner, more convinced of your value as a person.

SITUATION: My husband is so good-looking and so much fun that women fall all over themselves when he is around. And he flirts with all of them.

ANALYSIS: Congratulate yourself that you had what it took to interest such an attractive man—and you still have it. Let those other women eat their hearts out. You, too, might consider strengthening your self-image.

SITUATION: He is not paying as much attention to me as he used to. I'm beginning to wonder if there is another woman.

ANALYSIS: There is no reason for jealousy yet. But it is an indication that you should work on yourself and the relationship. There comes a plateau in almost every marriage when a husband and wife tend to take each other for granted. You can change this by courting him again. Shower him with lots of Positive Reinforcement. Let him know how much you admire him, how well he has done, how sexy he is.

SITUATION: He said he was going on a business trip. When I called him, a woman answered when the hotel connected me with his room.

ANALYSIS: This is cause for alarm, but don't jump to conclusions. There may be a perfectly innocent explanation. You might have been connected to the wrong room.

3. *If your jealousy is rational, decide what you want to do about it.*

What you have to do is control yourself—at least for the moment. As Yale University psychologist Peter Salovey says, "Getting angry, blowing off steam, eating a pint of ice cream all serve to make you feel worse. They keep attention on yourself and how upset you are." Instead, you should focus your attention on the situation and how you want to handle it.

Acting As If is effective first aid for jealousy. If your situation resembles that of the woman who called her husband at the hotel and found a woman on the other end of the line, bite your tongue and put on a smiling face when he comes home. No matter how jealous you are or how guilty you believe he is, Act As If everything is normal. This puts you in control and you have choices.

You may want to wait for a few days or a few weeks and see what develops, or you may want to choose an appropriate time and tell him what happened. Explain that you were upset when a woman answered his hotel-room phone. Stay calm, be reasonable and don't accuse. Simply tell him that if he has an explanation, you will feel a lot better.

Therapists usually recommend this course of action. "A well-integrated, emotionally mature person would confront the offending mate," wrote Dr. Phillip Polatin in the journal *Medical Aspects of Human Sexuality*, "and communicate his or her feelings and decide on a satisfactory conclusion to the problem to reduce tension and suffering."

This is excellent advice, but when you are being eaten up by jealousy, anger and self-pity, a rational discussion before bedtime or even the next morning calls for an almost super-human degree of control and composure. It is wise to put a cushion of time between the event that evoked the jealousy and any discussion of it. Therapists have found that people who Act As If for several days or a week come to feel more secure, act more rationally and regain control of their feelings.

When you feel that you can control yourself, then bring up the matter. You will be able to maintain your calm and composure and control the discussion.

Now, let's go back to Shari. If Shari had observed Rule One and decided to Act As If she were not jealous, chances are that she would have been in more control of herself by the time Irving got home. He had had a long day and was probably looking forward to a quiet evening and an early bedtime. She would have been wise to allow him to enjoy that quiet evening instead of tossing an emotional bombshell at him. After all, there was no rush.

There are usually two approaches to a delicate subject like this. The first would be for Shari to have asked him point-blank, "What were you and Donna doing at The Plaza last Tuesday?" But a direct question like this comes across as accusatory. It puts the other person on the defensive, even though he may be completely innocent. And there goes your rational, civilized discussion.

The second approach is to bring up the subject in a nonaccusatory way. She might have said, "You'll never believe this, but I was bitterly jealous of you the other day for about thirty seconds."

Irving's response would have probably been puzzlement.

"I went to The Plaza to have tea and saw you and Donna. I immediately decided you were having an affair. Don't ask me why. But sanity returned and I realized the two of you must have been talking business, so I didn't stop to say hello."

She could follow this up with a kiss and a hug. "It made me realize how much I love you."

What could he say? "I love you, too." And he would almost certainly have followed it up with "You were right about the business appointment. We were meeting the new client I told you about, the one who wants to switch his business to us."

Irving would have been amused and flattered. Shari would have been reassured and would not have revealed herself as vulnerable or needy. Their relationship would have been unaffected or, just possibly, strengthened, because Irving would be so flattered by her thirty-second attack of jealousy.

But what if Irving really had been having an affair with Donna? He would have denied it, and probably told Shari the same story about an appointment with a client. But it takes a master of deception, a skilled actor, to come across as believable in a situation like this. If Irving had been fooling around, he would have been totally unsuspecting, since several days had passed since he and Donna had met at The Plaza. Now, hearing that Shari had seen them would have come as a shock, and that instant of shock would have been betrayed in his eyes.

No matter how fast he recovered and how glib his explanation, Shari would have homed in on that trapped look in his eyes and known the truth. Unless she wanted to believe him. Sometimes the truth is too cruel to take in all at once. It might have taken several more confrontations before Shari was ready to accept the truth. Fortunately, Irving was a true and faithful husband.

## STAY IN CONTROL

If you are convinced that you have real cause for jealousy, what do you do? You try as hard as you can to stay in control of your emotions. When you are jealous, someone else is dictating how you feel. It is a form of emotional slavery with you as the slave and your husband as the master. He makes you feel jealous. Jealousy by itself is seldom a reason for major life changes. But it can be a symptom of a union on the verge of disintegration.

This is a time to go slow. Start a Basic Diagnostic List. This will give you insight into yourself and your marriage. What do you really want? What are your goals?

At the same time, you could work on two Worst-Case Scenarios. The very worst that could happen if you accused your husband of infidelity, and if you just kept your mouth shut and let things drift. The very worst if you separated or divorced, and if you did not. Don't take any drastic step until you have completed the Basic Diagnostic List. By then, you may have realized that it was all in your mind, or you may understand that your marriage is threatened. Whatever lies ahead, you are now prepared for it. You have thought about it, your emotions are under control. Now you can take constructive action.

## RESTORE YOUR SELF-ESTEEM

While it is helpful to understand how to cope with jealousy, it is even more important not to let jealousy poison your life. And there is only one way to do that—strengthen your self-image and increase your self-esteem.

If you have done humiliating things like going through your husband's pockets or wallet while he is asleep or checking to make sure your significant other is really working late at the office, then you are too jealous for your own good, and your self-image is way too low.

It is time to get to work, to develop confidence in yourself as a valuable and desirable woman. You can start out by working on this variation of the Basic Diagnostic List. Your first version might go like this:

| Assets | Liabilities |
|---|---|
| great cook | jealous |
| good housekeeper | feel inadequate |
| good mother | not interesting |

It would seem that your liabilities outweigh your assets. You are probably not doing justice to yourself. Think a little harder. What about looks, generosity, kindness, sense of humor? There is no mention of sex here. How do you rate yourself? Inhibited in that area?

When your lists are complete, start Acting As If. Act As If you are not jealous, Act As If you are confident. Act As If you are lovable. And Act As If sex is your favorite after-dinner treat. All this may take a little Previsualization at first, but you will be surprised at how natural it begins to feel.

Is this a guarantee that a straying husband or significant other will see the error of his ways? Not at all. But your self-image will definitely improve. There are no guaranteed happy endings. It may be when you have thought through your particular situation, you will decide you do not want to continue the relationship, but you will have made your decision on the basis of factors other than jealousy. And you will be self-confident enough to face whatever the future brings, because whatever it is will be for the best.

Is jealousy one of the self-defeating traits that can be transformed into an asset? Absolutely. A little jealousy can add spice to our lives and make sex more exciting. It makes us value our partner more highly. It can teach us about our emotional needs and spur us to do something about our shortcomings. But it can be an asset only if we learn to control it, instead of letting it control us.

# Chapter Sixteen

# ACQUIRED BEHAVIORS

## Those Rotten Little Habits

NO ONE IS perfect. We all have at least one habit or mannerism that drives people up the wall, as well as acquired attitudes and fears that block us from getting the most out of life. It may be a tendency to swallow your words so that listeners keep saying, "What? What was that you said?"; it may be an unconscious habit like constantly tapping your foot; it may be an acquired fear that makes you freeze up when you have to speak in public; it may or may not be related to a self-esteem deficit, but it definitely affects your image—for the worse.

Whatever it is, you were not born with it. It is not a genetic predisposition, but simply an undesirable trait or mind-set that you have acquired along the way. Why not get rid of whatever it is and let people perceive you at your best? These are not like the self-defeating traits that need only a little modification to neutralize or turn them into assets. They can and should be rooted out like weeds.

We are not usually conscious of our rotten little habit or mind-set. If you cannot think of one that you have, don't jump to the conclusion that you are flawless. As you read this chapter, you may become aware that you share a certain disagreeable behavior. If so, you are halfway home. You can begin to erase it from your personality. If you don't find one, it might be worth taking the time to make the following four checks, just to make sure that you really are without fault.

1. Make a list of the annoying habits of family members and friends. Chances are that you are guilty of at least one of them. "What we dislike most in others is generally what we dislike most in ourselves," says Dr. Marion Lindblad-Goldberg, "but it is easier to see these negative traits in others than to see them in the mirror."

2. Ask your nearest and dearest if they have noticed any little imperfection in you. If they reel off a laundry list of petty faults, just smile and forgive them. After all, you asked. And they probably did pinpoint one behavior that made you wince.

3. Go into a supersensitive mode for a week. Observe how people react to what you do and what you say. Watch their facial expressions and body language. One woman became aware that she constantly interrupted people as she observed the faint frowns and the tightening of the lips when she broke into conversations.

4. Make out a variation of the Basic Diagnostic List using the following headings:

WHAT DO I WANT IN LIFE?
WHY DON'T I HAVE IT?
HOW CAN I CHANGE THAT BEHAVIOR?

When Jocelyn, known behind her back as "Mrs. Know-It-All," adopted the supersensitive mode and worked on a Basic Diagnostic List, she discovered that she was constantly turning people off by her "I know best" attitude.

The clues? First, she spotted Eve and Molly raising eyebrows at each other when she told Selma that she had chosen the wrong kind of carpeting. "The only decent carpeting," she had been saying, "is made by the PQRS Company. If you had only asked me, before spending all that money," she lamented. And then she saw the raised eyebrows. She also noted that Selma had assumed a look of exaggerated patience.

When Jocelyn finished her Basic Diagnostic List, she realized that if she were to have any close women friends (which she very, very much desired), she would have to stop informing them that they could have chosen better carpeting or a better pediatrician. She also became conscious that "If you had only asked me . . ." was a phrase she repeated over and over. It was a hard pill to swallow, but she understood that her desire to impress people with her superior knowledge was a turnoff and stood in the way of making intimate friends.

Most of these acquired traits fall into three categories—physical mannerisms, speech mannerisms, attitudes and fears. In the following pages, I give examples of each category and recommend the appropriate psychological tools for getting rid of them. It is impossible to discuss every conceivable unpleasant trait, but these examples will serve as a guide to subduing other unwanted acquired behaviors.

## PHYSICAL MANNERISMS

These are the easiest habits to break, once you become aware of them. Most of these mannerisms are unconscious. The examples here should sensitize you to your own actions, but it would not hurt to ask your nearest and dearest if you have any of these or similar habits. Just in case.

### Nail-Biting

Most people see nail-biting as an indication of indecisiveness, lack of control and weakness. This disagreeable habit cannot be concealed, since nails bitten down to the quick cannot be hidden or grown back overnight. Unless you religiously wash your hands before nibbling, you are opening yourself up to everything from the common cold to a rotten fungus infection—and even worse. The nail-biter may be extremely attractive, but her Halo Effect will be negative. And if she gnaws at her nail in public, her Halo Effect will be disastrous.

CURE

*Negative Reinforcement:* Use the rubber-band bracelet, a good hard pinch or any other discouragement that you may find effective to break the habit.

In addition to that immediate punishment, whatever you decide on, try to think of ways to forestall your nibbling. Here are three suggestions:

1. Wear gloves as much as possible, at night as well as during the day and especially when you are alone and might give in to the need to nibble.
2. Use that bitter concoction that parents paint on children's nails to discourage them from biting.
3. Invest in frequent professional manicures. Both the cost of the manicure and the sensation of biting polished nails can act as deterrents.

*Positive Reinforcement:* If a week goes by without a nibble, reward yourself. Make the reward something you really want. This way, when you backslide, you will regret it even more because you won't have that new sweater or theater ticket.

*Previsualization:* See yourself with beautifully manicured hands and strong handsome nails. See yourself holding a champagne glass with those hands, and see other people admiring your beautifully manicured nails. See yourself holding a small baby and admiring her little pink nails, and thinking that yours are just as beautiful. Make up your own beautiful-hands scenarios where you, the heroine, are always displaying your well-kept nails.

## Nose-Picking

This is a real nasty, so disagreeable to observe. One week I counted the number of nose-pickers I spotted in neighboring cars as I waited for traffic lights to change. Thirty-five! They were almost evenly divided by sex, eighteen men and seventeen women. It seems to be a favorite pastime. I see people busily picking their noses as they wait in line at the supermarket checkout or waiting to cross the street, in all kinds of public places.

I was not counting nose-pickers for the sake of counting nose-pickers. This came about after I had lectured before a group of businessmen. One of them had caught my attention as he diligently probed one nostril and then the other. After the lecture, he came up to thank me—and insisted on shaking my hand. This sensitized me to the trait.

Nose-picking is unsanitary, unattractive and can lead to infection. And it is hard to think of a way to present a worse image to the public. Do yourself a favor and stop. At least, promise yourself you will only do it behind closed doors—with clean hands.

CURE

*Negative Reinforcement:* I favor a tough one, something that hurts. How about giving five dollars to a worthy charity every time you indulge in this rotten little habit? And don't consider yourself that worthy charity.

It might be a good idea to carry a little packet of tissues in your pocket or handbag, so that you have absolutely no excuse for sticking your finger up your nose.

## Face-Fingering

I have a friend who, after her face-lift, could not seem to stop feeling the hairline scars behind her ears. Her hand would go up to her ear every few minutes. Just for a second. It was like a nervous tic. I finally asked if her ear hurt. She looked blank.

"Why do you say that?" When I told her, she could hardly believe me. She had been absolutely unaware of what she was doing.

If you are always touching your face, smoothing your eyebrows, scratching your nose, rubbing your eyes or picking at that zit that you squeezed last night, you project a twitchy, nervous image that makes other people uncomfortable. If you doubt me, just visit the zoo and watch the monkeys pick, pick, pick at themselves and each other. It may be acceptable grooming behavior for monkeys, but who wants to sit across the table from a monkey at lunch?

CURE

*Negative Reinforcement:* See Nose-Picking. Face-touching is nowhere near as disgusting. I suggest fining yourself a quarter for each face-touch. Put it in a piggy bank and when you have broken the habit, treat yourself to a facial. You deserve a reward.

## Hair-Fiddling

Some people just cannot stop fiddling with their hair. They twirl it around their finger, they twist it or they pull on it. Twirlers and pullers are usually quite unconscious of their actions, but other people are not. It projects a poor image. Even worse, dermatologists warn that pulling and twisting can cause baldness.

CURE

Since this tends to be an unconscious habit, you have to do something to make you realize what you are doing, before you can apply a Negative Reinforcement. You might try wearing a turban or a cap or a kerchief, anything that will cover your hair. It is also a good idea to ask your family and friends to help you by signaling unobtrusively when you start fiddling with your hair.

*Negative Reinforcement:* Try the old standbys—the rubber

band and the pinch, if the threat of baldness is not enough to stop you right here and now.

*Reinforcement List:* Carry a little notebook and each time you become aware that you are playing with your hair, make a note of the time and place. You may discover that you fool with your hair in certain situations and environments, or when you are tired or nervous. Once you have determined this, you can make a conscious effort to leave your hair alone in these situations.

## Foot-Tapping

This mannerism, a constant foot movement, is one that can drive people up the wall as the foot-tapper taps away at the movies, in church, at the dinner table, almost anyplace.

Like the hair-twirler, the tapper is usually not conscious of what she is doing, so she must find a way to sensitize herself to this irritating behavior. Ask your friends and family to help you, by letting you know when you do it.

*Negative Reinforcement:* Years ago when I was teaching at Hunter College, one of my psychology students, who was a foot-tapper, attached small bells to her shoelaces. This proved very effective. The whole class was rooting for her. And as the number of times those little bells tinkled decreased over the semester, she received huge gobs of Positive Reinforcement as her classmates congratulated her. This was a very effective—and pleasant—form of Negative Reinforcement.

You might try this or come up with an imaginative deterrent of your own. And there are always those standbys—the rubber band and the pinch.

## VOICE AND SPEECH MANNERISMS

We slip into all kinds of speech habits that annoy people. A producer I once worked with had an annoying habit of swallowing the last two or three words of every sentence. She would start out clearly, but then seem to run out of the energy to project her voice. This meant you either had to guess what she wanted or keep asking, "What did you say?"

She had no idea she had this annoying habit until one day she asked a panel guest if he had trouble hearing. "Indeed I do," he replied. "I have trouble hearing you. You swallow your words so that they become unintelligible, and I can't understand a thing you are saying." She was shocked. I am happy to report that she immediately got in touch with a speech coach who helped her overcome this mannerism.

## The Voice That Alienates

Women with a grating or childish, whining voice, the screecher and the mumbler all project a disagreeable image. Unfortunately, people are seldom aware that they are mumbling or that their voice reminds people of a honking goose. If you suspect you may have a voice that alienates, I suggest you check yourself with a tape recorder. Tape yourself while reading aloud and while you chat with friends on the telephone.

(I am sure you know that it is illegal to record a telephone conversation without informing the other person, so it is better to use a regular tape recorder rather than your answering-machine recorder. A voice-activated tape recorder is best because there are no long pauses while the other person is talking.)

CURE

*Positive Reinforcement:* If you have an off-putting voice, a few sessions with a speech therapist or coach would be a worthwhile investment if your budget will stretch to it. It will also make you feel good about yourself as you find your voice improving from session to session. A pleasant voice is a great asset and worth the time, effort and expense it may take to acquire.

Listen to people on television and in films and assess their voices. Which ones do you like? I am not suggesting that you try to imitate someone else's voice, but simply try to determine what it is that makes a speaking voice appealing.

## The "Like" and "You Know" Syndrome

Some people pepper their speech with "ers" and "ahs" and "ums," with "you knows" and "likes." These nonwords are just noise. They project an image of a lazy and imprecise thinker. Check yourself by tape-recording your telephone chats with friends, and by asking people you see daily if you are guilty of these nonword sentence fillers.

If you can't seem to say more than a few words without interjecting "you know" or "like" I suggest you get to work promptly on remedying this, since it is truly an undesirable habit in both business and social contexts.

CURE

*Negative Reinforcement:* Ask your family and friends to signal when you start on the "you know" and "like" route. I suggest a really meaningful punishment to root out this behavior. Maybe a dollar for every slip. And donate the money to a favorite charity (not yourself).

## ACQUIRED ATTITUDES AND FEARS

### Interrupting

Some people have a seemingly irrepressible urge to prevent others from finishing a sentence. They butt in with "Oh, that reminds me of the time . . ." "Are you sure it was a Tuesday? I heard it was a Monday . . ." "My brother-in-law says . . ." "No, no, you've got it all wrong. This is the way it happened . . ."

Why do people interrupt? Usually, it is because they want to be the center of attention, or they disagree vehemently about what is being said, or want to show that they are better informed. Whatever the reason, it is an immature behavior that shows a lack of courtesy and control. Children interrupt. Something comes into their heads and they say it, until they are taught that this is unacceptable behavior. Unfortunately, some people grow up without having learned to curb these impulses.

The interrupter may be unaware of how annoying she is, but she usually has a subliminal feeling that something is wrong, that she is not being welcomed into the group as warmly as she would wish. Run this little check on yourself to see if you are guilty of interrupting.

1. Do you find yourself plunging in impulsively with your ideas when someone else is talking?

2. Do you raise your voice to drown out the other person?

3. Do other people in a group often react to whatever you are saying with stony silence?

If you answered yes to at least two out of the three questions, you are an interrupter and you should apologize. You can train yourself to stop, think and listen before speaking. Before you open your mouth, ask yourself if what you want to say is going to contribute to whatever the person is saying. If it is, be courteous and wait until she has finished. If you have not been able to resist interrupting, it is important to apologize to the speaker.

CURE

*Negative Reinforcement:* See the *"Like"* and *"You Know"* *Syndrome* above. And again, ask friends and family for help. Tell them you are trying to cure yourself of interrupting and ask them to speak up and say "You're interrupting again," when and if you do.

## Gossiping

This can be so much fun. There is the kick you get when you tell Judy that Sophie is having an affair with Betty's husband, or that you've heard that Jonathan was dropped from the bowling team because he made a pass at the Women's League captain. Everyone likes to hear the latest tidbit, but not everyone likes the gossiper. People don't trust a gossiper. They wonder what she is saying about them behind their backs.

Gossiping is a dangerous trait. At the office, a reputation as a gossip is a black mark against you. It is not going to help you get ahead if you are known as one of the group that gathers at the coffee machine to dish. Your superiors will see you as someone who wastes time and may endanger office morale. It is better to be known as someone who can be trusted to keep her mouth shut.

It is okay to listen to gossip (you might learn something), but if it is damaging or hurtful, you don't want to be associated with it, so try to put a stop to it. Say something like, "Oh, I really can't believe that" or "It's really none of our business" and walk away.

CURE

*Negative Reinforcement:* Promise yourself that you will stop. Gossiping is not one of those unconscious habits. You know very well what you are doing, so the penalty should be high. My suggestion is that you fine yourself $5 an item and donate the money to charity. Don't cheat. If you do, you will be cheating yourself twice. First, you will not break the gossip habit, and second, you will have broken your word to yourself.

*Worst-Case Scenario:* Make out a scenario every single time you pass on a bit of gossip. For instance, if you told people that you saw Betsy having drinks with the boss after work, try the following scenario:

What is the worst that can happen to Betsy if this gets to the wrong ears? The boss's wife, for instance.

What is the worst that can happen to you if the boss learns that you were broadcasting this little tidbit?

What if the boss was telling Betsy that she was being promoted? And what if she will be your new boss?

## The Head-in-the-Sand Syndrome

You wonder if your husband is having an affair, but you tell yourself that he would never do that. All those late nights are because business is so bad or so good. Those telephone calls when someone hangs up as soon as you answer are probably mischievous kids.

You have that little spot on your face, that scaly little spot that just won't heal. It fits the description of a squamous-cell cancer that you read in a magazine, but you tell yourself it's nothing, just a little irritation.

You found some little plastic packets of white powder in your son's drawer when you were putting his clean underwear away. It crossed your mind that it might be cocaine or something. But then you thought "Oh, Harry would never be involved with drugs." You say nothing and do nothing.

You'll be sorry.

Sorry, when your husband breaks the news that he is moving out.

Sorry, when your gynecologist takes one look at you and says, "I think you should see a dermatologist as soon as possible. Do you want me to make an appointment for you?"

Sorry, when the police call and say your son has been arrested for dealing drugs.

Who did you think you were fooling? You did not even fool the woman in the mirror. Why did you refuse to face the evidence? You played ostrich and buried your head in the sand, because you did not want to face unpleasant facts. As a result, your marriage is on the rocks, you have advanced skin cancer and your son is involved with drugs.

The sad aspect of all this is that these unhappy outcomes might have been prevented if you had taken action. In any case, you would have done your best to prevent them or handle them, and might not now be faced with a broken marriage, a skin cancer and a son on drugs.

CURE

*Worst-Case Scenario.* The best cure for fear is to face it. Make out a scenario for all those nagging little fears that you keep trying to evade. What if your husband is thinking about divorce? What should you do? What do you want to do? Preparation is more than half the battle.

What is the worst that could happen if you had the dermatologist look at that spot on your face? If it was malignant, it would have been taken care of earlier.

And what is the worst that could happen if you had told your husband about those plastic packets of white powder, and the two of you had done something about the situation?

*Act As If:* After making out these scenarios, you will understand that you have to face the facts and do something about it. "But I don't have the courage. I don't dare," you say. That may be. And in that case, Act As If. Act As If you were strong and logical and capable. You will be surprised at the effect you will have on others. You *will* make a difference. For the better.

## You Can't Say No

One of the first words babies learn after "mama" is "no." Children have no difficulty in saying "no." But girls who said "no" from birth through adolescence somehow turn into women who can't say "no." When someone asks them to make a cake for the bake sale, to edit the library newsletter, to pull together the statistics on attendance at the town meetings over the last decade, to be chairman of the program committee, they say "yes" even though they haven't had time to get their hair done in months.

Did you ever stop to wonder why they always asked you? Why don't they ask some of the other women? The fact, plain and simple, is that the more tasks you agree to take on, the more

tasks people will dump on you—especially if you are both efficient and effective. There are other people in the world. Let them
take on some of these duties. Give yourself a break. Learn to say
"no."

CURE

*Basic Diagnostic List:* Use these headings:

WHAT I ENJOY DOING
WHAT I DETEST DOING
THE TWO PROJECTS I'LL TAKE ON THIS YEAR

You have to establish a new way of responding to requests.
Make up your mind just what you want to do—and can do.
Decide to do the tasks that give you the most satisfaction. Perhaps you can work on the program committee, and you can
have the whole family for Thanksgiving, but someone else has to
do Christmas. And that's it.

*Worst-Case Scenario:* If you are a woman who can't say no,
because you feel indispensable, I suggest you work on a scenario
of the worst that could happen if you did say no and the best that
could happen if you said Yes to whatever it was. This should
cure you of feeling indispensable.

*Previsualize:* Obviously, it hurts you to say no, because you
have had little or no practice. Spend half an hour a couple of
times a week, previsualizing how you will regret your inability
to do whatever it is. See yourself being gracious in your refusal,
explaining that the demands of your family and job do not permit you to take on anything more at this time. And, above all,
previsualize yourself sticking to your guns.

*Negative Reinforcement:* If, by any chance, you weaken and
say yes, make yourself call back immediately and say that you
cannot possibly do it. You have looked at your schedule and you
cannot fit it in. Then thank them for thinking of you, and sit
back and indulge in a sigh of relief.

## Empty Threats

My daughter suggested that I include this rotten behavior. "I hear mothers threatening that there will be no television for a week, that the youngster will not get his allowance, that the trip to the beach is off because their child has been disobedient or whatever. But it's all talk," Lisa said. "They never follow through. What does this teach children?"

One thing it teaches children is that they can get away with all kinds of behavior. A child loses respect for authority when a threatened punishment is not imposed. The parent must learn control and not let her momentary anger or concern lead her to threaten punishments that are out of proportion to the crime.

CURE

*Negative Reinforcement:* For the mother, not the child. Do not threaten a punishment on the spot. If you start sounding off, stop! Stop, take a deep breath and tell your child something like, "I'm really upset about this behavior. I want to talk to you about it when we get home/ after your friends leave/as soon as I finish feeding the baby." And at that time, sit down calmly, talk about his or her disobedience or freshness or whatever and explain that this is unacceptable behavior. Make it clear that next time it happens, there will be an appropriate punishment. And make it clear what the punishment will be. Let it fit the crime. Both mother and child will be happier.

## Fear of Public Speaking

We were all born with a wonderful capacity for making ourselves understood. The infant has a whole range of crying behaviors that indicate clearly whether it is tired or hungry or uncomfortable. As adults, some of us lose that ability to express ourselves, especially when it comes to speaking in front of a group.

Fear of public speaking afflicts some of the toughest career women in this country as well as your next-door neighbor, the Girl Scout leader who goes into a blue funk at the prospect of having to welcome the parents of her Scout troop to the annual picnic.

There are two effective approaches that will help you overcome this fear. The best way to overcome it is to speak in public until it becomes second nature. A friend of mine, who was determined to overcome her fear of public speaking after a disastrous appearance before a kennel club that had asked her to speak about obedience training, volunteered to serve as a docent at a local museum. This involved giving talks to tour groups as she conducted them around the galleries.

At first she was flustered and shaky, but she kept at it week after week. Today, a year later, she is a poised and effective speaker. "I never would have believed it," she says, "but I actually enjoy it. When I know I have captured people's attention, it's a very special feeling, a high."

But most women have little reason to speak in public and when they have to, it is crisis time. It need not be. You can conquer this fear.

CURE

Half the battle is preparation. You must know what you want to say. Think it through and write it down, making sure that you have covered the necessary points. Then deliver your speech to your mirror. If it is too long or too short, work on it some more and deliver it again.

*Previsualization:* Once you have what you are going to say clearly in mind and you know how long it will take, previsualize yourself delivering the speech. See yourself walking up to the podium, pausing for a moment to let the applause die down, turning to thank the person who introduced you and then delivering the speech. The more often you go through this Previsualization routine, the more relaxed you will feel on the day. If you are a novice at this, I suggest going through your Previsualization at least five times.

*Act As If:* If possible, arrange to visit the hall or room where you will be speaking. Find out where you will sit. Walk up to the podium. Look out into the room and visualize it full of smiling anticipatory people. Smile at your imaginary audience, pretend to take a sip of water, look out at the audience—and speak.

If it is not possible to have a trial run, go through the motions at home. Walk into a room, walk up to the pretend podium, et cetera, et cetera. Deliver your speech to a mirror. Don't let yourself speak too fast. Emphasize the important points. And look out at the audience, not at your text, although it is perfectly all right to pause for a second and check the test. Two or three such Acting As If rehearsals will make you completely familiar with what you are going to do and say.

You may feel nervous on the actual day, but Act As If you are perfectly at ease, happy to greet your audience and eager to share whatever it is you have to say with them. They will perceive you as a perfectly poised and effective speaker.

## You Are on Your Own

It is impossible to do more than describe a handful of typical rotten little habits and hang-ups in a single chapter. If, as you finish reading this chapter, you think, "But she didn't talk about how I can stop my habit of putting people down or criticizing," you don't need me to tell you. The examples you have just read show you how to use the various techniques alone and in combination to eliminate an undesired behavior. You have the tools and you can do the job.

# Part Four

# ☑ THE STRESS FACTOR

## Converting It Into Your Strongest Asset

Stress can be a positive force in your life, or it can mash you into a quivering pulp. It can expand your mind and enrich your personality, or it can turn you into an anxiety-ridden, hopeless, angry individual. It can contribute to, or block you from, success.

Hans Selye, the father of the concept of stress, divided it into eustress and distress. Eustress is an "up" feeling and distress a downer. The mountain climber experiences eustress when he reaches the peak of Mont Blanc after a long, hard climb. The surgeon feels this positive stress when she successfully completes a difficult operation. The student feels it when she gets a high grade in a physics course in which she had to struggle to comprehend the material.

The woman who is let go in a reorganization, and is overcome with fear that she will not find another position, experiences distress, negative stress. When a car cuts in front of you on the freeway and you lean on your horn and feel like strangling the driver, you are in the grip of negative stress.

Some people have a fear of flying, despite statistics showing that plane crashes account for fewer deaths than automobile accidents do. These people prefer to drive if at all possible. They feel in control at the wheel of a car. And that sense of control is the difference between eustress and negative stress. The more control you have over the situation, over your actions and emotions, the more positive stress you experience and the better you feel. Lawyers tend to handle stress better than businessmen. This is because they usually have a chance to prepare their cases thoroughly, to check previous cases, find loopholes, work out their strategies. The more they prepare, the more control they have and the better their chances of success.

Businessmen, on the other hand, usually have to handle problems as they appear. They rarely have time to sit back and plan their strategy or consult experts. They have to make their decision and act then and there. Their lives are more stressful because they have less control over the situation.

However, many businessmen—top executives with huge responsibilities—relish stress. They see each problem as a challenge and look forward to dealing with it. And as they handle each challenge successfully, their feeling of control and competence increases. When some 1,000 top executives of Fortune 500 companies were evaluated, it turned out that these extremely competitive men who were under almost constant stress were healthier and happier than the average man. The researchers concluded that each stressful situation that these men had coped with during the course of their careers had increased their competence and confidence. It was these strengths that separated them from other equally hardworking men and put them at the top position in their companies.

These findings apply to women as well. In a recent study,

some 1,000 women executives who were married and had children reported very little negative stress in their lives. They found the challenge of the combined home and career demands invigorating. They felt in control, sure of themselves and their decisions, and they had high energy levels. In contrast, 40 percent of women in nonmanagement positions reported they felt stressed and fatigued more than half the time. They blamed this negative stress on workplace tensions and problems over which they had no control.

Negative stress drains us of energy. Positive stress unleashes energy. When you can turn negative stress into positive stress, it is like being given a new lease on life.

Dr. Selye was convinced that it was one's attitude toward challenges that determined whether the stress was perceived as positive or negative. A self-defeating reaction to stress transforms it into negative stress. "Adopting the right attitude," he said, "can convert a negative stress into positive stress."

When you understand the chemistry of stress and what it does to your body and mind, you realize why it is important to handle stress in a positive manner. Perhaps you have been stuck in stop-and-go traffic for the last twenty minutes. You will be late for your appointment to show a house to a prospective buyer. This is stress.

Your brain detected the stress immediately. It released hormones that stimulated the pituitary gland to releases a hormone that stimulated the adrenal cortex. The adrenal cortex then released cortisol, a hormone that helps the body adjust to stress. The more often this complicated procedure is triggered, the more damaging it is to your health. The hormone onslaught can play havoc with your body if it is frequent and uncontrolled. It increases your blood pressure, reduces your immunity to disease and shuts down your digestive system. It can bring on a heart attack or a stroke.

Sitting in your car, you may have decided after the first five minutes that "This is out of my hands. There is nothing I can do about it. I'm going to relax." As you inch along, you listen to the news on the radio or make out a shopping list or plan next summer's vacation.

This is a positive way of coping with stress. You realized there was nothing you could do about the situation and turned your attention to something else instead of stewing about something over which you had no control. The minute you relaxed, your brain got the message. The glands shut down their hormone production, and your body was only minimally stressed.

On the other hand, you may have sat there with a white-knuckled grip on the wheel, cursing your bad luck, telling yourself that the appointment will have to be postponed for days, and you will probably lose the commission you hoped for. In this case, hormones continue to flood your system. Your heart is pounding, your head aching, your blood pressure stratospherical. Every nerve and muscle is sensitized for action. It is the same "fight or flight" response that energized our caveman ancestors into action when menaced by a wild beast. If this surge of adrenaline is your typical way of reacting to stress, it would be wise to modify it. Today's "wild beasts" are more effectively controlled by brain power than by brute strength.

The everyday, nitty-gritty stresses like getting stuck in traffic are harder on body and soul than life's major stressful events like moving, losing a job and divorcing, according to a study conducted at the University of California. Although these major changes can be extremely stressful, they are one-time traumas. Eventually the new house becomes home, you find a new job, the divorce is final, and life goes on.

But the inevitable frustrations and setbacks of everyday life when the vacuum cleaner conks out just as you are getting ready for company, or you learn that your suitcase has gone to San Francisco and you are in Santa Fe—these go on and on. If it is not one thing it is another, day after day. And there is nothing you can do about it. Although you have little control over such annoyances, you can learn to handle your reactions to them and cut the negative stress in your life way down. As I said, it is not the stress-making incidents that tear us apart, it is the way we react to them.

Once you learn to handle stress, it can be your greatest asset. Not only will you get along better with people and feel more in control of your life, you will discover enormous stores of energy you never knew you possessed.

In the following chapters, I suggest psychological tools that will help you turn negative stresses into positive ones. These techniques will work with any stresses in your life, not just the ones I use as examples. I also warn against the "quick fix" remedies for stress that are not only self-defeating, but can be deadly.

*Chapter Seventeen*

# WORKAHOLISM

---

## The "Virtue" That Can Kill

---

MY DAUGHTER TEASES me and calls me Queen of Busy because I work so hard. I always have. Fourteen-hour days are not unusual as I fly around the country, but I thrive on it. The challenge of going from city to city, of turning from writing to lecturing to television, often in the course of one day, is stimulating to me.

People often ask why I work so hard and I tell them it is because I love what I am doing and I believe it is useful. They say, "Oh, you must be a workaholic." But I am not.

Work is only one part of my life. I have always made time for family. When Lisa was young, this called for a considerable balancing act, but between us, Milt and I managed to be there for all her important occasions. And weekends were always friend-and-family time. Now that I am alone, I still keep my weekends free. I often make flying trips to Iowa to be with Lisa and my grandchildren, but most of the time I go to the farm and just relax and catch up with myself. I read a novel or a new mystery. I walk through the fields down to the brook, weed my herb garden, check out the local antique shops and chat with the neighbors on our little dirt road. When I leave for the city Sunday night, my batteries are completely recharged and I am raring to get back to work.

Contrary to popular belief, not all people who work hard are workaholics. Fortunately, no more than 5 or 10 percent of the population are workaholics. I say "fortunately," because workaholics are not happy people. They are victims of perfectionism and suffer the stresses of the damned.

I discussed perfectionism earlier and explained how this self-defeating trait erodes one's self-esteem, because the perfectionist always falls short of her own expectations. Workaholism is another form of perfectionism and seems to be even more stressful than the never-good-enough thinking of the perfectionist. The basic difference between a perfectionist and a workaholic is that the perfectionist thinks nothing she does is ever good enough, while the workaholic believes that her work is superior, but that she should always do more of it. One strives for unattainable quality, the other for unattainable quantity. The result for both is a constant state of debilitating stress.

## PORTRAIT OF THE WORKAHOLIC

We tend to think of workaholics as men, but women are equally prone to workaholism and suffer more from its effects. Women workaholics experience more stress in their relationships and have higher divorce rates than their male counterparts, according to a study at the University of Texas involving 1,500 women. For both men and women, however, workaholism is a highly stressed lifestyle, as the following thumbnail portrait of workaholics shows:

- Workaholics come to work earlier and stay later than anyone else. They routinely take work home at night and on weekends.
- They tend to be rigid and resist change stubbornly.
- Workaholics tend to become estranged from their families, because they are always too busy to spend time with them. For the same reason, they have no real friends.

- Workaholics find it difficult to establish good relationships with their colleagues at work, and seldom show sensitivity or warmth to those below them in the pecking order.
- Workaholics resist delegating responsibility, which means they spend too much time on relatively menial tasks.
- Workaholics think they are wasting time when they are not working. They see no reason to change. If anything, they believe they should work harder and do better.

The truth is that they *should* do better. They may believe that they are both the brains and the backbone of the organization, but a fourteen-year-long study by psychologist Charles Garfield of the University of California found that despite the long hours they put in, the quality of the workaholic's output seldom measures up to that of her peers.

Most make a great splash when they start on the job, but their careers level off early. "They tend not to make a major impact," Garfield reported. "The workaholic never makes the discovery, writes the position paper or becomes the chief executive officer." And starting in their thirties or early forties, workaholics become increasingly susceptible to stress-induced illnesses, and are especially prone to heart attacks, alcoholism and drug addiction. At this period, family problems also tend to escalate and come to a head. Divorce is common and suicides are not unusual.

## WORKAHOLICS VS. ACHIEVERS

There are other men and women who are extremely hard workers, who work equally long hours and who thrive—both personally and professionally. They are the CEOs, the achievers. They have warm relations with their colleagues. They hire highly competent people and give them a lot of freedom and responsibility. They are close to their spouse and children, value friendship and make time for fun.

The achievers have hectic lives, but they love every minute of what they are doing, and they feel in control. This sense of control and their enthusiastic approach to life are key factors in their general well-being. Their stress levels are low, and the incidence of heart attacks and other stress-related ills among these top achievers is close to the norm. There is another important difference between the workaholic and the achiever. The workaholic is often addicted to work not because she wants to win fortune or fame, but because no matter what she did as a child, her parents always said, "You can do a lot better than that if you try." Psychologist Barbara Killinger, who treats workaholics, says that "typical workaholics are not driven to overwork by economic necessity. They gradually become addicted to work in a compulsive drive to gain approval." The workaholic's goal, whether she realizes it or not, is to please her parents, even if they are no longer on earth.

The extremely hard worker, on the other hand, is working toward specific goals that she has set herself—an advanced degree in astronomy, passing the state bar exam, revising the town's zoning laws, or opening her own restaurant. We all need goals. We all feel better and more fulfilled when we do our best. That does not mean doing things perfectly, but simply giving them our best try.

## GEARING DOWN FROM WORKAHOLISM

But what about workaholics? Are they really doomed to a life of dissatisfaction with themselves and their achievements, to a life of stress because of impossible, perfectionist goals? Not necessarily.

The wise workaholic would do well to throttle down to a pace closer to the norm. This is not the easiest of goals. It usually takes a shock to get a workaholic to understand what she is doing to herself and her family. A heart attack brings some workaholics face-to-face with reality. Sometimes a divorce or being fired will do it. In Betsy's case, it was a frightening, blinding headache that forced her to reevaluate her life.

Betsy ran her interior-decorating business from a charming Victorian house she had remodeled. Her office and model rooms were on the ground floor and she lived upstairs, which meant that she never left her work behind at the end of the day. She worked fourteen to sixteen hours a day, seven days a week. It was a hectic life—trips to designer showrooms in New York, appointments with clients, keeping up with new design trends and dealing with workmen.

She had recently branched out into corporate work, designing executive suites. This had meant doubling her staff, whom she expected to match her pace and intensity. When they did not, she became curt and critical. The result was a constant turnover, as employees soon had enough of the criticisms.

One client who had become a friend asked, "Why do you do this? You're driving yourself crazy. Why don't you go back to your private clientele? You know you hate doing those offices."

"Why should I?" Betsy said irritably. "I've made a big investment in staff and time to service corporate clients. It's just beginning to pay off."

But Betsy's increasing impatience and sharpness, a direct result of fatigue and stress, had begun to affect her relationship with clients. They drifted away to other decorators. She redoubled her efforts to attract new clients, introduce fresh looks, find new sources, until one day she had a blinding headache accompanied by blurred vision. She went to her doctor, thinking her blood pressure was a little high.

"I'm going to put you in the hospital for a couple of days for tests," he said after examining her.

"I don't have time," she said impatiently. "Can't you just give me a prescription in case I get another headache?"

The doctor made it clear that she should make time. Two days of tests revealed nothing intrinsically wrong. "Take a month off," the doctor instructed. "Get away. Forget about work. And when you come back, I suggest you rethink this business of working crazy hours seven days a week. If you keep it up, you are asking for a heart attack or a stroke."

This struck home. Her father had had an incapacitating stroke and lingered on, helpless, for months before he died. She took the doctor's advice and went on vacation. Lazy days on a sunny Caribbean island gave her time to think. She realized that her manner with clients had become brusque and impatient. She also faced the fact that while she was working night and day, her overhead had increased so that she was not clearing significantly more money than before. It was time to change.

## A PROGRAM FOR TURNING DOWN WORKAHOLIC STRESS

A year earlier, Betsy had attended one of my executive seminars on "Making the Best of Your Worst" as the guest of a corporate client. She still had the Psychological Tool Kit tucked away in a desk drawer and now she took it out. She started with the Diagnostic List and was surprised by what she learned about herself. In the first place she had no real goals. Her Master List was revealing.

| Best Qualities | Worst Qualities | Goals |
| --- | --- | --- |
| artistic | too tense | to excel |
| meticulous | too brusque | |
| hard worker | work too hard | |

"I could not believe I had no other goals in life than to excel at my work," she said later, "and that was really a cop-out. I had to put *something* down on the list and it was all I could come up with. It was an eye-opener to understand that one of my best qualities, working hard, was also one of my worst!

"And I had so many worst qualities! Impatient, irritable, dictatorial, always in a rush, disorganized, curt. It was hard to decide on the three worst."

She decided to work on a variation of the Diagnostic List, a Goal Analysis. She had to establish some goals for herself besides her desire to excel. She changed the format a bit, dividing her goals into those she really wanted and those she thought she should want. When she later wrote to me about this, I thought it an excellent idea because it forced her to analyze her goals. One of the great things about the Psychological Tool Kit is that it can be adapted to your own needs and situation.

Betsy's Goal Analysis read like this:

| What I really want | What I should want |
| --- | --- |
| friends | be better organized |
| more interesting life | more clients |
| more time to create | larger staff |
| more fun | more recognition |
| fresh ideas | larger office |

Her Goal Analysis showed that what she wanted was a fuller, more rewarding and pleasurable life. The goals she thought she *should* have revolved around her professional life. She had spent the last few years working toward what she thought she should do instead of what she wanted to do.

It is hard for workaholics to change, especially if their workaholism stems from a childhood in which whatever they did was not enough for their parents. But a Goal Analysis can concentrate one's energies on achieving a desired goal so strongly that it helps you override old habits and psychological mind-sets.

Simply getting one's goals down on paper seems to enhance your chances of achieving them. Nearly 87 percent of the men and women participating in a study on achievement had no real goals in life. Ten percent of them had goals, but had never crystallized them to the extent of putting them down on paper. Only 3 percent had goals and had also written them down. And this 3 percent achieved fifty to one hundred times more in their lives than the 10 percent who had goals but had never put them in writing.

Betsy remembered what her friend had said about dropping her corporate clients. With her new perspective, she realized that her friend knew what she wanted better than she had known herself. The idea of restricting her work to private clients again was suddenly very appealing. To have time again really to get to know a client and her lifestyle, to give the client an attractive and comfortable setting that reflected the woman and her family—this was the professional goal that she really wanted.

## THE WORKAHOLIC RELAPSE

Once she had completed her existing corporate commitments, Betsy began to worry that she had made a great mistake. She felt uneasy, almost guilty that she was not working hard enough. Workaholism does not subside easily.

She stayed later and later in her office. To keep busy, she would review everything the assistants did, going through their files. When she came across a preliminary sketch for a client's dining room, calling for walls covered in a scarlet silk damask, she was furious. The next morning she called the assistant responsible for the project into her office. "This is absolutely wrong," she stormed. "You must be out of your mind. Mrs. Eliot wants a quiet, conservative look."

"No, she doesn't," the assistant contradicted. "Her mother-in-law just came back from Japan with three bolts of the scarlet silk. She decided she would like to make a splash in the dining room. And if you don't trust me, I don't want to work here." With that, she stalked out of the office.

Betsy was shocked to realize that she had slipped back into working long hours and trying to control every detail. Her assistant's reaction was a strong Negative Reinforcement against Betsy's resurgent workaholism. She apologized and promised to stop second-guessing.

To reinforce her promise, she made out a Worst-Case Scenario, writing down the very worst things that could go wrong if she did not monitor every detail of the business, and the very worst things that could go wrong if she did. The results were enlightening. Her scenarios showed that things would go fairly smoothly whether or not she constantly rode herd on them. It forced her to face the fact that she was really attempting to stay busy twelve and fourteen hours a day.

She pulled out the Goal Analysis she had made earlier, and decided the time had come to work on her personal goals of bringing more pleasure and people into her life. If nothing else, it would distract her from her compulsion to work for the sake of working.

It took time. She started by joining an amateur theater group. Later she began inviting favorite clients to lunch or dinner. Little by little she brought more friends and more fun into her life. She caught herself backsliding now and then, but she learned to shrug her shoulders and continue her fight against workaholism. She still works harder than most people, but these days she also plays harder. Gradually, she moved away from the extreme of workaholism to the rewarding norm of the executive who relishes both work and play.

Today she understands that her workaholic drive to do more and more resulted not only in accomplishing less and less in terms of quality, but was alienating clients and friends. These days she has just enough stress in her life to keep her stimulated and happy. She has reached the realm of the golden mean.

# Chapter Eighteen

# ANXIETY

## How to Seize Control of Your Fears

MOST ANXIETY IS part of the human condition. Everyone has a certain amount of fear of the future. You worry that you might lose your job and not be able to make the mortgage payments. You fall in love with someone wonderful and question whether it will last. We are nervous wrecks before our annual physical, because we fear that no matter how well we feel, the doctor is going to find something wrong. And when the exam is over and he says, "You're in great shape," we are euphoric, as if we had narrowly escaped disaster.

A certain amount of anxiety is beneficial. It is the anxious people who figure out better ways of doing things. If we were not worriers, we would still be living in caves. In fact, this kind of anxiety is based on sheer primitive superstition. We worry because we are afraid that if we don't worry, the thing we worry about will happen. Put that way, it sounds absurd, but it is exactly why most of us worry, and it is not all that absurd. So much of life is beyond our control that we have developed this superstitious attempt at control.

We make all kinds of attempts to stave off misfortunes. Many people rely on "magic" talismans. For instance, if I spot a penny on the sidewalk, I always pick it up. Someone told me that it is luckier if the penny is heads-up, so I feel even better when I find one that is heads-up. This is sheer superstition, and I am supposed to be an intelligent woman! But that deep-down lurking superstition says, "Who knows? Maybe it will help. At any rate, it won't hurt."

Years ago, I talked with the scientists involved in the moon shot. On the day of the shot, they told me, they all wore their lucky things—their lucky T-shirt, their lucky coin, their lucky slippers, whatever. Despite the precision of the entire operation, the scientists wanted luck, too.

This seemingly ridiculous reliance on "lucky" charms is simply a way of controlling anxiety. If we believe it works, it works. For instance, you are waiting for a bus on a cold winter's day. The bus doesn't come and doesn't come. You light a cigarette. And as you take the first draw, the bus comes into sight. Next time you wait for a bus, you think you know how to get it to come. You light a cigarette. If it comes, the superstition is established. If it doesn't, you shrug your shoulders. But the next time you wait for a bus, you try again.

Remember the Operant Conditioning study of rats that I wrote about in Chapter Five and how powerful Intermittent Reinforcement can be? This is exactly how our superstitions become established. If the bus comes every third or fourth or fifth time that you light up, this provides Intermittent Reinforcement and you feel that there is a connection between lighting up a cigarette and the arrival of the bus. You feel you have a degree of control, even though your common sense tells you it is nonsense.

## A MINEFIELD OF DISASTERS

There are many people whose anxieties are far from the norm, and no innocent little superstition is going to give them a feeling of control. They are on the extreme edge of the bell curve of anxiety, and are victims of "free-floating anxiety," an amorphous, yet all-encompassing cloud of fear and foreboding.

For them, life is a minefield of impending disasters—illness, chimney fires, unemployment, impotence, meteorites, global warming, fungus infections, old age, infidelity, flat tires, inflation, deflation, leaky plumbing, earthquakes, you name it. Their energy is sapped by worry about what might happen.

Most of them turn to money, our substitute gratification for the prepotent needs, as the magic talisman that will shield them from the caprices of fate. They squirrel it away against a cataclysmic deluge (their concept of a rainy day).

Since they are never sure their talisman is magical enough, they keep on saving and saving even after they have provided themselves with a generous buffer against disasters. Like those mice who scrabbled endlessly in the sand for nonexistent food, they become victims of the Secondary Gain Trap. They subject themselves to lifelong stress because of their belief that with enough money they can control the future.

This kind of uncontrolled anxiety turned one couple's life into a never-ending struggle to prepare for the worst. Nancy and Art deprived themselves of life's pleasures because they were so intent on defending themselves against its dangers. Theirs had been a marriage of like to like. On their honeymoon, they decided they would always play it safe, living frugally and saving so as to be ready to cope with any troubles, major or minor, they might face. They made their wedding checks the nucleus of their defense fund.

It seems strange to think of saving money as self-defeating, but it can be. There is a vast difference between putting aside a reasonable amount of money for emergencies and saving so much that you deprive yourself just because it may rain on your life one day.

By the time their thirtieth wedding anniversary rolled around, Nancy and Art were more than ready for any rainy days that might come their way. Their stocks were blue chips, their bonds high-grade. And they had a cash hoard buried under the back steps. Still, their anxieties ruled them. A headline about an earthquake in Japan or an avalanche in Switzerland filled them with foreboding. When the washing machine gave up the ghost, they were sure the rest of the household appliances would follow suit.

When disaster did strike, there was no way money could protect them. A trailer truck jackknifed and hit their fifteen-year-old automobile, completely demolishing it and killing Nancy and Art instantly.

"It's such a shame," their daughter said. "I'm glad they had enough to take care of any rainy days that might have come their way, but I wish they had spent more of it on enjoying the sunny days—living more comfortably, living in a nice house in a pleasant neighborhood, going out with friends, just plain having fun. They were always so serious, always worrying, always thinking of more ways to save.

"My husband and I are very comfortably off, since they left everything to us," she said. "And I assure you we intend to spend it like normal people. What we have done is contribute a significant proportion of their estate to the Red Cross in their memory. I think they would have liked to have their money help others cope with disaster."

## BRINGING ANXIETY BACK TO THE GOLDEN MEAN

The all-encompassing sense of anxiety felt by Nancy and Art is at one extreme of the anxiety bell curve. Anxiety shadows these people's lives. At the other extreme are the people I think of as zombies. They passively accept whatever life hands them and never look to the future.

The people in the bell curve of normality have varying degrees of anxiety but are able to control their worries and fears. They understand that while life can be malignant at times, it can also be benign. Their anxiety level is within the area of the golden mean.

Normal anxiety is a positive rather than a negative trait. It is an advance-warning system, encouraging us to think of better ways to do things, to plan ahead and to avoid future stress.

Excess anxiety, anxiety that seems to pervade your whole life, is a sign that you should do something about something. Three of the most common anxieties that haunt women are:

1. I might lose my job.
2. My husband might die and I would not have enough money to live on.
3. I might be in an automobile accident that leaves me a paraplegic.

These are valid fears. There is nothing unreasonable about them. All three, however, reflect fear of helplessness and a lack of self-confidence. They reflect an inner belief that they cannot handle these crises and will end up homeless, or on welfare, or worse.

And yet, people surmount such crises every day. Think of Carol, for instance, who set up a day-care center to become financially self-sufficient after her divorce. Think of the hundreds of thousands of physically disabled people who refuse to let themselves become helpless. Think of all the people who have lost their jobs in the last few years and have either found new jobs, become self-employed or worked out a new lifestyle and new ways to cope.

The way to start dispelling your anxieties and bolstering your self-confidence is to diagnose exactly what that "something" that you should do something about is. Once you pinpoint the source of your anxieties you are halfway to mastering your negative stress.

## THE THREE-STEP METHOD TO CONTROL ANXIETY

Start out by making a variation of the Condensed Diagnostic List along these lines:

| Strengths | Weaknesses | Fears |
|---|---|---|
| 1. | 1. | 1. |
| 2. | 2. | 2. |
| 3. | 3. | 3. |
| 4. | 4. | |
| 5. | 5. | |
| 6. | 6. | |

This will help you decide which anxieties to tackle first. The very act of putting your three greatest fears down on paper can make them seem a bit less frightening. As you try to isolate your fears, you will undoubtedly discover that many of them are so unlikely that you will not even consider listing them. And you will realize that others are beyond your control. Yes, the nuclear plant down the river might blow up. You might be in a building that is bombed by some fanatic, or you might be struck by lightning or the earth might be hit by an asteroid, but there is nothing you can do about these possibilities. Just tell yourself that the chances of their happening are very slim and then put them out of your mind.

Follow the same procedure and time frame as the standard Condensed List. When you work on the Master List, put down your single greatest fear.

Now that you have faced your anxieties and pinpointed your most harrowing anxiety, the way to bolster your self-confidence is to decide how you would handle it if it came true. What would you do?

Which of your strengths will help you cope? Which of your weaknesses might make the situation worse? Think of ways to turn those weaknesses into strengths. You have the psychological tools that will help you do this as well as the law of Reversion to the Mean, which will work behind the scenes.

The second step is to make a variation of the Worst-Case Scenario for your worst anxiety. This will make you think about your options and give you a sense of control. It will force you to face it and think in concrete terms about what you can do to guard against its coming true and how you would handle it if it did.

If your greatest fear is losing your job, your Worst-Case Scenario might read something like the one below.

### I MIGHT LOSE MY JOB

#### WHY DO I THINK I MIGHT LOSE MY JOB?

I've heard there are going to be some cutbacks.

My boss is annoyed whenever I am ten or fifteen minutes late in the morning and he bawled me out the other day for taking long lunch hours.

Our sales have gone way down this year.

The new assistant is bucking for my job. They would not have to pay her as much.

| The Worst That Could Happen | What I Would Do If It Did |
|---|---|
| I lose my job. | Look for another job.<br>Tell people I'm job-hunting. |
| I can't find a job. | Look for part-time work.<br>Look for a temporary job.<br>Look in another city or area.<br>Get training that will make me more employable. |
| I run out of money and can't pay the rent. | Make an arrangement with the landlord.<br>Move to a smaller place.<br>Move in with friends. |

## I Might Lose My Job *(Continued)*

### What Can I Do About It?

Perhaps I should start looking for a new job, before I'm fired.

I should get to work on time and cut out long lunch hours.

I've been thinking about those pedometers we make. What if we worked out a deal with a manufacturer of jogging shoes? It could expand our market. Perhaps I should send the boss a memo about this.

### What Do I Want to Do?

I think the reason I'm always late and take long lunches is that I'm bored. Perhaps I should look for a new job.

At the same time, I want to stay right where I am. I know everyone and the routine is familiar. I'm nervous about the idea of starting all over again someplace new.

If the boss liked my idea about pedometers and told me to go ahead, I would feel more challenged.

I guess I should write that pedometer memo *and* look for a new job.

Take your time with this. Be as specific as you can. Decide whom you will tell that you are job-hunting, what kind of temporary job you would look for, which friends you would move in with, et cetera. The scenario is just to get you started thinking. The more time you spend on this, the more you will learn about yourself and the more options you will discover.

Pay particular attention to what you put under the heading *What Do I Want to Do?* You may want to move ahead and try something new, and at the same time be scared of change and want to stay exactly where you are. In this case, a second Worst-Case Scenario is indicated. What is the worst that could happen if you found a new job? The worst if you stayed put?

The third step in mastering a fear is Previsualization. Write down step-by-step exactly what you would do if the worst happened. This kind of Previsualization is an ongoing process. You will think of new ways to cope from day to day. Once you start thinking in concrete terms, your anxiety is reduced because you are dealing with realities and possibilities, not unfocused fears.

Now, let's look at the other two common fears that I mentioned.

## What if My Husband Dies and Leaves Me Penniless?

If you stay awake nights worrying about this, use the same three psychological tools. Here are a few points you might consider: Why are you frightened that your husband might die? Is there a health reason? Is there some way you can persuade him to take better care of himself? Or is there no real basis for your fear?

Death comes to all of us, but it is quite unlikely that your husband would leave you penniless. Have you discussed this with him? Are you familiar with the family finances? Have the two of you made wills? If not, this is something you should do as soon as possible.

What about insurance? If he does not carry any life insurance, this would be a good time for him to talk with an agent and take out a policy. If, for some reason, he is uninsurable, the two of you should discuss how you would manage in case of his death.

You might also take steps to assure your own financial independence. Well over half the married women in this country work today. There is nothing like your own job to make you feel secure. If you do not feel that you can work outside the home for one reason or another, think about doing volunteer work that could provide a stepping-stone to paid work if it should become necessary.

And Previsualize exactly what you will do from the moment your husband dies, what you will do about the funeral, the will, the house, where you will live, how you will live and what you will live on.

### I Might Be Disabled as a Result of an Automobile Accident

There will always be accidents. Just walking down the street exposes you to the possibility of accident. But why do you suffer from this particular anxiety? Is it because this happened to someone you know? That does not mean it will happen to you. Is it because of something you read? Again, this is quite unlikely to happen to you.

Use the same three techniques to put this fear in a rational perspective. In this particular case, make as many entries as you can under each heading of the Worst-Case Scenario except for the last.

When you come to *What You Want to Do About It,* your choices will probably be limited to one—I want to prevent it. Go on to list ways that you can try to prevent an automobile accident and then take the necessary steps. For instance, have you done everything you can to lower the odds against serious injury in an accident? Does your car have dual air bags, antilock brakes, adequate structural protection? Do you maintain it properly?

And you? Are you a good driver? If an accident is a major anxiety, enrolling in a safe-driving course may help lower the degree of anxiety. Your automobile club can probably recommend one. Is your insurance adequate and up-to-date?

The worst may not be as terrible as you imagine. If this is one of your fears, I strongly recommend you volunteer in a rehabilitation clinic where you can see for yourself how effective therapy is, and understand that even a severe disability is not the end of a good life. This will also help you in Previsualization, because this part of your previsualizing will be based on reality, rather than fearful imaginings.

## WHEN YOUR BRAIN SAYS "ENOUGH"

Once you get started on this positive approach, the Ripple Effect will set in, and little by little your confidence in your ability to cope with problems and misfortunes will increase and your stress will decrease.

At some point, after working on the Condensed Diagnostic List, the Worst-Case Scenario and Previsualization, you will reach the point where your anxiety is significantly reduced. You have faced your fears, thought them through, and decided how you would handle them. You have completely immersed yourself in whatever they are. Finally your brain says, "Enough! I don't want to dwell on this any longer." And you are free!

You have pushed your fears into the area of the norm. Instead of wallowing in useless, self-destructive anxiety, you have engaged in constructive thinking and planning about ways to prevent your fears from coming true and about what to do if they should come true. And this has freed your energies to get on with life.

# Chapter Nineteen

# ANGER

## Injustice Hoarders and Exploders

ANGER IS ONE of our most primitive emotions. It is the descendant of the rage reflex that primitive man shared with lower animals. It is also a "moral" emotion. Think back to the last time you were angry with someone. It was probably because you believed that something they did or said was unfair. The way you handled this perceived injustice governed the amount of stress you felt. You may have kept your anger to yourself and simmered inwardly, or you may have let it out in a burst of emotion harking back to that old primitive rage reflex, or you may have decided it was really not worth getting angry about and ignored the incident.

In which category do you belong?

Suppose your sister commented that the lawn of your new house was more crabgrass than grass and "you ought to do something about it." You've been spending every weekend working on the house, sanding floors, putting down new vinyl in the kitchen, papering and painting. How would you respond to her remark?

1. You feel like telling her off, but then you shrug your shoulders and think, "She wouldn't be happy if she didn't have some-

thing to criticize." And you laugh and say, "Oh, it's an equal opportunity lawn."
*Stress:* None to slight.

2. You bristle and think angrily, "Why does she always have to find something to criticize? We're knocking ourselves out working on the house. We haven't had time to even think about the lawn." You conceal your anger, however, and say, "We'll get to it one of these days." But inside you are seething and during the coming week, you keep stewing about her criticism. You are an Injustice Hoarder.
*Stress:* Medium-high to high.

3. But perhaps you snap, "Who asked for your opinion?" You tell her she's always poking her nose into other people's business and besides, her house is always a mess. You are an Exploder.
*Stress:* High to very high.

Both the second and third types of reaction are self-defeating. Your anger will feed on itself and infect other areas of your life. That evening, for example, Timmy may accidentally knock over his glass of milk, so you shout at him and order him to clean up the mess. As your anger escalates, you tell him he can't watch television for a week.

Normally, you would have said, "Oh, oh! Quick! Get the mop." And that would be that. But because you were still stewing over your sister's remark, you blew up again and imposed a punishment way out of proportion to the "crime."

Family relationships are particularly stressful because of their intimacy. We tend to treat our families more harshly and cavalierly than we do outsiders. We yell at our children when they drive us up the wall. On occasion, we may treat our husbands like enemies—and, for a moment, we may indeed think of them that way.

We expect these intimate flare-ups to be forgiven and forgotten, and they usually are. We understand that intimacy breeds tensions, and we take it for granted that the ties of love are strong enough to withstand occasional peevish tantrums. Most angry flare-ups within the family are like summer storms, over in minutes. But while they last, they are extremely stressful. Sometimes, however, anger goes underground. And grudges are held for years and years. Sisters don't speak to each other. In-laws stop visiting back and forth.

The same reactions are true in other relationships—with friends, with coworkers, with strangers such as sales people or telephone solicitors. The amount of stress generated by these reactions varies according to how you handle your anger.

## HOARDERS

Some people hold on to their anger as if it were precious. They hoard every perceived injustice.

"When we were supposed to be going steady in high school, he was dating Margie. . . . When Kim was born, he said she looked like a squashed tomato. . . . I hinted I'd like to go to New York on our anniversary, but he made reservations for Las Vegas. . . . We always have to go to his folks for Thanksgiving. He says it's too expensive to fly to Nebraska just to eat turkey and pumpkin pie. . . ." And on and on.

Hoarders go over their accumulated grievances the way other women inventory the pantry shelves or review their investments. Old grievances grow in importance almost as if they had been injected with a growth hormone. The suppressed anger becomes more virulent. And a time comes when relationships are poisoned by this anger that has flourished in the dark, like some giant toadstool.

The Hoarder herself pays a high toll in stress and stress-related afflictions. Studies have linked the repressed anger of Hoarders to a whole list of ills including breast cancer, hypertension, heart attacks, asthma, diabetes, fatigue, immune-system disorders and an unsatisfactory sex life.

## EXPLODERS

Some Hoarders become Exploders when the pressure of their anger becomes too great, just as a volcano will erupt when the pressure becomes too great. Some people are Exploders by temperament, but many Exploders are victims of an outmoded theory. There was a time, not too long ago, when many psychologists and psychiatrists considered it healthy to let your anger out. Blowing your top, they believed, rid you of this dangerous emotion.

"If I bottled it up, it would eat away at me," Exploders excuse themselves. "People who repress their emotions get ulcers and all kinds of things. But once I get things off my chest, then I'm fine."

Today we know better. "Catharsis, taking out your anger on the person you're mad at, doesn't lift the anger," says Dr. Diane Tice, a psychologist and stress-researcher at Case Western Reserve University. Anger that is expressed angrily begets more anger. Letting it all out is like throwing gasoline on a fire. The only healthy way to handle anger is to control it, and then either use it or forget it.

There will always be stresses over which we have no real control, and some of those stresses will produce anger. So what do you do? It is all well and good to understand the sources of your anger, but what can you do about it? How can the Hoarder get rid of the poisons she has been accumulating? How can an Exploder control her anger?

## WHO IS PULLING YOUR STRINGS?

The Hoarder must realize that what is done is done. You can't put Humpty Dumpty back together again. There is no turning back the clock.

The Exploder must realize that nothing is gained by letting it all out. There may be a fleeting sense of power as one shouts and carries on, but it is an illusion.

Both reactions are self-defeating and sometimes self-destructive. They increase the intensity of the anger and heighten the stress level. Hoarders and Exploders are like puppets; someone else is pulling their strings. When you permit someone to make you so angry that you hoard the anger or explode, you become helpless. The other person is controlling your behavior, not you. Is this what you want? Wouldn't it be better to be in control of yourself and the situation?

Some Exploders claim, "It's the way I am. There's nothing I can do about it." They are absolutely wrong. Both Hoarders and Exploders can transform their anger into an asset, into positive energy. All they have to do is decide they will be in control.

The psychological techniques that can help you control your anger are right here in this chapter. They can be used by both Hoarders and Exploders, and they work. There is no downside to them. You can dissipate self-defeating anger, channel productive anger and gain new energy. Your life will take on new and happier dimensions.

First of all, Exploders and Hoarders need a psychological tool that kicks in immediately to short-circuit their anger. Then they need one that gives them insight into themselves and the sources of their anger. Both are in the Psychological Tool Kit.

Operant Conditioning in the form of Negative Reinforcement and the Reinforcement List can be used to short-circuit anger. Negative Reinforcement will help put it on hold and gain time to get it under control. The Reinforcement List will pinpoint when and why you become angry and the effect—good, bad or indifferent—of your anger. This will reduce the number of anger episodes, lower the stress they generate and bring your reactions closer to the norm. If you have identified yourself as a Hoarder or an Exploder, I suggest you reread Chapter Five on Operant Conditioning. You will find Josie's use of the Reinforcement List to curb her temper particularly useful.

## DISTANCING MANEUVERS

It is important to put a few seconds, or even better a few minutes, between whatever has made you angry and your reaction, particularly if you are an Exploder. Remember, you have a choice; you can fight or flee. The wise woman will flee, temporarily distancing herself emotionally and, if possible, physically from the situation. She prevents herself from reacting before her anger is under control.

Simple but effective distancers that you might make use of are:

Drinking a large glass of water.

Counting to ten, an old but effective way to gain time.

Deep breathing. If you combine this with counting to ten, you gain time to think about how you are going to react and you gain a degree of control, since slow deep breaths have a calming effect.

Bending down to tie your shoe or to pick up an imaginary paper clip or a thread. This breaks eye contact, which tends to escalate anger. Another way of breaking eye contact is to blink rapidly, saying you have something in your eye. This has the benefit of removing you physically as you go look for eye drops or whatever.

Removing yourself from the scene even for a few minutes is even better. Go to the bathroom, or suddenly "remember" that you left something on the stove, or your favorite pen on someone's desk, or you have to call your aged aunt.

Best of all—if it is possible—is fleeing, getting away completely. Go for a long walk, or wash the car or weed the garden. Exercise is a wonderful way to work off stress, and it can cool down white-hot anger very efficiently.

Let me warn you against driving it off. In one study, 10 percent of men reported that when they were angry, they would jump in their car and drive until they simmered down. This is really dangerous. They put not only themselves at risk, but others as well. Neither their judgments nor their reactions are as reliable or quick when they are angry. When I read the report of that study, I started driving a lot more defensively.

Whatever distancing mechanism you use, this form of Negative Reinforcement will help you control your anger enough so that you can respond calmly to whatever the situation. You should then be able to confront the person and say something along the lines of "You know that made me angry. Why did you do that/say that/tell him that? I suppose you had a good reason. Would you let me know what it is?"

You can be icy cold. You can be assertive. You can be distant. The one thing you cannot be is out of control, because that means the other person will be in command, and that is enough to make you really mad.

## CHANGE YOUR FOCUS

Your next step is to change your focus and put the whole thing out of your mind, at least for the time being, preferably for good. Focus-changing will help Exploders simmer down, and is particularly important for Hoarders, who must resist the temptation to file away this new anger with all the others they have collected over the years.

This is simply another Negative Reinforcement. Force yourself to think about something else. Put the anger-making incident out of your mind.

Impossible, you say? "It sounds very sensible," one woman said at a lecture, "but I don't think it can work. When I'm angry, I'm not going to stop and think about a beautiful sunset or the latest international crisis. I'm too mad to think about anything else."

"It will work," I promised her, "if you just give it a chance. Your brain will be on your side." I explained that our brains can only efficiently handle one topic at a time, so introducing a new thought can derail or short-circuit anger.

If you are anger-prone, I suggest preparing a few subjects to focus on next time you have to control your anger. For instance, what would you do if you won the lottery? If you were going to buy a new car, what make would you get? What clothes do you need for your vacation?

## USING ANGER CONSTRUCTIVELY

When you are in control of your anger, you will be able to think logically about how to handle the situation. You may decide to forget it, or you may be convinced that you should take action.

There are times when anger should be expressed, and expressed forcefully. We should and must speak up about injustices and wrongdoing. But anger is only effective when it is controlled. Once it gets out of hand, even if you are on high moral ground, protesting the most blatant injustice, anger becomes self-defeating. People perceive you as overemotional, uncontrolled and possibly dangerous.

## SUBSTITUTING A NEW BEHAVIOR

It is not easy to adopt a new style of dealing with anger, but the Rehearsal Techniques can be enormously helpful. Acting As If and Previsualization will help you become so accustomed to controlling your anger that it becomes a completely natural and unconscious way of reacting to a perceived injustice.

Previsualize yourself reacting calmly to something that makes you angry. Think back to the last time you were angry. Then, step by step, visualize how you could have handled the situation better. See yourself using two or three distancing tactics to gain time before reacting. Visualize yourself telling that person what made you angry and asking why he or she did it. Then visualize how that person would have reacted to your response.

This way, you will be ready to Act As If you were calm and controlled the next time you are faced with an anger-provoking situation.

## THE ENERGY PAYOFF

Once your anger is under control, you can use it or decide that the incident was not worth getting angry about. Note that I say "control," not extinguish. When brought into the area of the golden mean, anger is useful and carries a minimum burden of stress.

Think back to the bell curve of Reversion to the Mean. At one extreme are the meek, and while they may inherit the earth in some utopian future, right now the meek are treated more like door mats than heirs to the planet. At the other extreme are those who cherish and nourish their anger. They are in a constant state of stress. Anger devours energy the way a Rolls-Royce devours gasoline, and it wears us out, both physically and emotionally. But the great majority of us are inside the bell curve. We get mad now and then, and sometimes get carried away by our anger. Most of the time, however, we manage to control ourselves.

Anger has its own continuum. Uncontrolled anger is self-defeating in every aspect. It alienates people and exhausts you because it consumes so much energy. But you do not want to get rid of your anger completely. All you want to do is move it closer to the norm. Anger, when controlled, can be useful, a concentrated source of energy that can be a dynamic force for the better. Anger creates the momentum that spurs social reform, that results in better schools and better teaching, that preserves the environment, that saves the whales, that fights racism and sexism.

To turn anger into an asset, first of all, you have to turn down the heat. Don't let the fire rage out of control. And second, you have to decide what you will allow yourself to be angry about. Don't waste energy on petty incidents. There are times when a shrug of the shoulders is the healthy response to a perceived injustice.

"I feel like a new woman!" a librarian in her fifties told me. She had attended one of my seminars on Reversion to the Mean and had used the psychological tools I describe in this chapter to change her habitual injustice hoarding.

"You are a new woman," I responded. "You are bursting with energy, you have a new, positive outlook. You are doing more and getting more out of life."

She stared at me. "How did you know that?" she asked.

I smiled. "Because you told me so. You told me that you no longer squirreled away everything that made you angry. You told me that now you try to either ignore the incident or to bring it up in a quiet manner and let the other person know that you are angry and why. This means that you no longer waste all that energy on hoarding anger. Of course you are getting more out of life."

# Chapter Twenty

# SELF-DESTRUCTIVE BEHAVIOR

## The "Cure" That Makes Things Worse

PLEASE THINK OF this chapter as a road sign, one that says DAN-GER! in flashing red letters. In these last chapters I have outlined constructive ways to turn self-destructive reactions to anxiety, workaholism and anger into positive coping mechanisms, and to bring the stress itself into the area of the norm. These psychological techniques can be used to transform all kinds of stress into fresh energy safely and effectively.

In this chapter, I want to discuss attempts to deal with stress that can be self-destructive. Even deadly. It is important that you know about them, because at first they may seem to be effective and alluring. But they are far worse than the stress itself. They can drag you down into physical and psychological hells, and unfortunately, are often our first remedies. I am talking about attempts to calm anger and anxiety, to cushion loneliness, to deaden the pain of failure and the loss of love with alcohol, drugs, gambling, sex, even food.

## HOMEOSTASIS

These attempts at self-medication, for this is what they are, all too often end up as full-blown addictions. They start as attempts to achieve homeostasis, a kissing cousin of the law of Reversion to the Mean. The difference between them is that Reversion to the Mean, which works to bring behavior within a normal range, will never lead you to extremes. Homeostasis, on the other hand, which is the body's attempt to establish psychological and physical stability, can lead to lethal excess if you interfere with the process.

Let me give you a medical example of homeostasis. It used to be that we routinely took aspirin to lower a fever. Now we have learned that we are better off letting the fever run its course. Fever is the body's attempt to cure itself, to achieve homeostasis, and it usually succeeds.

Aspirin may reduce the fever, but it interferes with the body's effort to fight the infection that caused the fever. So these days, many doctors do not prescribe aspirin unless the fever becomes dangerously high, and then aspirin and other treatments are called into use.

We also have an innate drive toward emotional and psychological homeostasis. When you try to handle emotional stress by self-medication, the medication may relieve the stress temporarily, but it may interfere with that innate drive to reach homeostasis by bringing the cause of the stress under control. The symptom may have disappeared for the moment, but its cause still exists, and you can eventually find yourself in real trouble.

Have you ever noticed, for instance, how many angry people are seriously overweight? There is a cause-and-effect mechanism at work here, a usually subconscious attempt at self-medication.

We associate food with comfort and warmth. Almost everyone has comfort foods. Most of us have memories of being given special treats as children when we were ill or hurt ourselves. I remember being given cocoa with a marshmallow floating in it when I got home from school on bitterly cold days. And all my life I have associated cocoa and marshmallows with feeling cozy and coddled. To this day when I drag into the apartment late at night, exhausted after a delayed cross-country flight, I go straight to the kitchen and make myself a cup of cocoa, wishing I had a marshmallow to put in it.

In the same way, an anger-prone man who has just blown his top at his secretary because he found a typo in a memo, or cussed out the mechanic because the fender bender cost more than he expected, will head for the refrigerator or a candy counter to get back into homeostasis. He will not think of it in these terms. He will simply crave a cheese sandwich or a candy bar. Eating makes him feel comfortable and brings him back to emotional equilibrium. His anger subsides and all is well with the world—until the next angry outburst. And that next time, he may need to eat more before he calms down. This is homeostasis at work. It is also how addictions are born.

Eating becomes a form of self-medication for some angry people. It deadens their stress for the moment, makes them feel more relaxed, and brings them closer to the norm. But the attempt to achieve emotional homeostasis through overeating soon gets out of hand. The overeating results in obesity, with all its attendant medical risks.

## MEDICATING THE MIND

People think of drug and alcohol dependency as symptoms of psychological problems. They are, but they are also the result of attempts at self-medication. The user is trying to medicate her mind, to reduce her stress and feel more like herself.

The use of drugs and alcohol does not start as a conscious attempt at self-medication. What happens is that one day there is a crisis of some sort: you lost your job . . . your mother is seriously ill . . . you totaled the car, etc. You feel just awful. A friend says, "You need a drink." So you have a drink, and perhaps you have another. Soon, you feel a little better.

The alcohol does not eliminate your anxiety. What it does is distance you from the way you feel, muting the stress. The effect is similar to the way you would feel if your best friend was having root-canal dentistry. You sympathize with her pain, but you do not feel it the way you would if it were your tooth.

The situation that is causing your anxiety still exists. In fact, it usually becomes worse, since you are not doing anything constructive about it. Little by little, you increase your intake of alcohol to keep your miseries at a comfortable distance, but the anxiety increases. And you drink even more. Soon, any setback sends you to the bottle to anesthetize your anxieties. It becomes harder and harder to achieve homeostasis. The time comes when no matter how much you drink, you are no longer able to push your stress into the comfort zone, into the area of the norm. Your attempts at self-medication have turned into an addiction. You have become an alcoholic.

## WHEN YOU HAVE IT ALL

The same thing is true of drugs. Did you ever wonder why so many famous athletes and film and television stars take cocaine? They have everything on earth—riches, recognition, success. Why should they need cocaine or other chemical mood-changers?

There is a reason. We have a pleasure center in our brains. If you attach an electrode to the pleasure center of a rat's brain and you allow the rat to push a bar that stimulates that electrode, that rat will stimulate itself to death. When a human being achieves success, there is a rush of adrenaline that stimulates the same part of the brain. The successful person feels on top of the world. It is a completely natural high. And, like the rat, we want more.

But success is capricious. Even when you are on the top of the heap, there is always the nagging worry that you may not be there tomorrow. An actor may work for years and years without recognition, and then suddenly she is in a play or film that makes her a star overnight. She feels great, but the next morning she starts to worry. What if another role like this never comes along?

Even the biggest stars suffer from this anxiety. I talked with Henry Fonda shortly before he made *On Golden Pond* and he told me that all of his life, once he had completed a film, he was always concerned that he might never be offered another role. He always worried that he would find himself on the shelf for good.

It may be even worse for star athletes, because there are so many pitfalls that they cannot control. The outfielder runs, the sun is in his eyes and he does not catch the ball. The football end gets hurt, and he is out for the season. The championship golfer's swing is off on the crucial day. There is always the worry that they will never again taste the joys of success.

No matter how great a star they may be, there are always periods when no one is jumping up and down and telling them how wonderful they are. And this is when cocaine and other drugs sneak into their lives. Drugs stimulate that pleasure center in the brain and, like the rat in the experiment, too many of them stimulate themselves to unconsciousness and even death as they seek to experience that high over and over again. Cocaine makes them feel on top of the world again—briefly.

Drug use is usually not premeditated. Perhaps one night when a star performer is feeling down, cocaine is offered after dinner and she tries it. She feels wonderful again, because the anxiety that has been dogging her is deadened.

So the next time she has the jitters and the willies and feels her career is at a dead end, she tries cocaine again. And it works. Suddenly everything seems possible again. The sun will rise the next morning. She will be offered the role of her life. She will finally meet the man who will truly love her.

All she is doing is trying to achieve homeostasis, to bring her feelings closer to the norm. But the euphoria does not last. She needs more and more, and she needs it more often. Whenever she feels down, she doses herself with a line of coke. She tells herself she can't go dragging around like a failure. She has to appear confident and successful. Soon she is dependent on her drug of choice.

The time comes when it does not work as well as it used to. She cannot get herself back to stable-state emotional normality no matter how much she uses. And one day we read about her breakdown or death in the tabloids.

This kind of drug use, as we all know, is not confined to those in the public eye. We all have our own particular demons that stress us out from time to time and make us vulnerable to the "friend" who wants to introduce us to drugs.

The same downward curve from occasional use to addiction occurs when sex is used to achieve homeostasis. Sex is an expression of love, a source of pleasure. It is exciting. But it can get out of control if it is habitually used as a medication for stress.

The bored housewife (and boredom can be very stressful) takes a lover and experiences all the tremors and delights of sex as it used to be. The excitement and the sizzle are back, making her feel wonderful. But all too soon, it becomes the same old thing all over again. There is no more sizzle. No satisfaction. No comfort.

So she takes a new lover to regain that hectic delight that dispels her deadly boredom. After a while, her appetite for sex becomes insatiable. No one man can provide the excitement that she craves.

It may not be boredom that leads to sex addiction. Men and women turn to sex to overcome depression, anger, fear, all kinds of anxieties. It provides wonderful surcease for a time, but it can become an addiction that leads to an empty, lonely life.

In all these instances, the attempts at self-medication no longer work. The easy ways out—food, alcohol, drugs, and all the rest—end up as traps. And then the users go through hell trying to free themselves from their addictions. Ask any former alcoholic or drug addict. They never feel secure. One false step, one weak moment and they are trapped all over again.

## INSTEAD OF SELF-MEDICATION

So, back to stress. The healthy and effective way to handle stress is to modify your reactions to it in the ways that I outlined in the previous chapters.

There are times, however, in everyone's life when we are confronted with crises, tragedies, or life-changing events that are hideously stressful and emotionally painful. There is no way to soften the pain and loneliness of the loss of your job or the death of a spouse or child.

These are such savagely brutal happenings that alcohol or drugs may seem particularly alluring, but their promise is false. They only intensify the stress and prolong the misery. The only way to come to terms with such major crises is to live through them, to understand your reactions, and let nature do her work.

In Part Five, I discuss ways to help yourself survive these life-changing crises, using the psychological tools that will bring you safely back to homeostasis, that blessed area of the golden mean.

# CRISES AND TURNING POINTS

## When the Very Worst Happens

Early on in this book, I wrote about hearing two women complain about how unhappy they were with the rotten cards life had dealt them, and how they wanted to throw them in for a whole new hand. I hope by now I have convinced you that the characteristics we may consider drawbacks can be moved along the continuum of behavior, so that their negative aspects disappear.

But what about the really rotten cards life deals us? What about the tragedies like the death of a husband? These are not susceptible to modification. There is no nudging death into some "not-quite-dead" state.

Things happen to us at random—horrible, terrible things. They can happen to anyone at any time. We believe they will never happen to us, but they do. My husband died of cancer. My neighbor's little girl, four years old, was killed in an automobile accident. Just the other day, a television producer, his face white and hands shaking, told me that his "flu" had been diagnosed as full-blown AIDS. One of my neighbors, a thirty-seven-year-old executive, came home a few weeks ago and told his eight-months' pregnant wife the company had declared bankruptcy. They owed him a month's salary and there would be no severance pay.

Every major life crisis represents a loss of some kind. It may be a loss of trust, of belief, of a way of life or life itself. When we suffer such losses, we are stunned, momentarily paralyzed. All we can do is ask, "Why me?" There is no answer to that question. As the bumper sticker proclaims, "Shit Happens." But you don't need to stay stuck in that shit. Your life has changed, sometimes overnight. It will never be the same again. But it can still be good.

If someone had told me this when my husband died, I would have been angry at the person spouting such nonsense. But it is true. While there is no way of escaping your grief and fears, your loneliness and anger, there is a way of living through these crises without allowing them to defeat you. Just as fire tempers steel, the crucible of grief can make you a stronger person.

When I open a lecture this way, I can actually see a wave of disagreement flow through the audience. Women draw their chins in, exchange looks, roll their eyes. They radiate disbelief and skepticism. I know exactly what they are thinking.

*My husband is dead. I'm supposed to change that? . . . I was let go last month when the corporation downsized to the tune of 2,500 people. I'm not going to find another job in this economy. . . . My husband wanted a divorce. Now I feel like a second-class citizen. My old friends have dropped me. . . . I'm seventy-eight and I hate it. And there's no way to turn back the clock. . . .*

They are right. There is no way to turn back the clock. It is impossible to return to the status quo of yesterday, last week, a year ago. But, in time, it is usually possible to change the painful situation in which you find yourself for a better one.

Remember when I told you that stress can turn out to be your strongest asset? The stress you undergo in these situations can spur you to make your life whole and vital again. It can increase your understanding and compassion, challenge you and fulfill you. I know. I, too, have lived through the loss of love.

It is not easy. Nothing about loss is easy, whether it is the loss of a job, of a loved one, or of a network of friends. All losses have a common denominator. Loneliness.

Loneliness is a world of its own. It is like being on a planet where everyone is involved in life, except you. Where no one seems aware that you even exist. It is an empty feeling, a hungry feeling, an almost unbearable inner ache. Some women describe it as an actual physical pain. And when you ask where it hurts, they touch their hearts.

By the time I finish my lecture, the skeptics in the audience are nodding in agreement. They come up to me, eager to share experiences—their own and those of others. They reassure each other that, of course, life must go on. And if and when it becomes necessary, they will draw on their strength and the knowledge I have shared with them.

In the following chapters, I discuss ways to banish the loneliness inherent in all tragedies of loss, as well as ways to master self-defeating reactions to crises. Once you take control, you will be able to restore balance to your life and reach that golden mean, where sorrow becomes serenity and bitterness acceptance. You will open new doors on life and once again function as a whole and vital person. A stronger woman.

*Chapter Twenty-one*

# THE LOSS OF LOVE

## When Death Steals Your Husband

THE VERY WORST that happened to me in my whole life was the death of my husband. For months and months I went through life on automatic. I was a walking pool of tears. My good sense seemed to have gone down the drain, and I made crazy mistakes. No matter how brave I tried to be, no matter how I forced myself to go through the motions, to pursue my career, to be a good mother and grandmother, my heart was not in it. I felt hollow, and I was desperately lonely. The only reality in my life was that Milt was gone.

I was convinced that nothing would ever be right again, so firmly convinced that I could have sworn on my daughter's head that life would never be worth living again. But I was wrong. Little by little, almost without my realizing it, life did get better. One day I found myself laughing. It was as if I had walked out of the shadows into the sunshine. A part of me will always be missing. But I am happy again, and a little wiser.

Several months ago, as I was preparing a lecture on bereavement and thinking back to those first dark days, I had one of those "Aha" experiences when you suddenly gain a new insight.

Enough time had passed since Milt's death so that I had the perspective to understand that my ability to enjoy life again had been the result of the phenomenon of Reversion to the Mean and my own behavior, as I unconsciously used a number of familiar psychological techniques to get through my days of grief and mourning.

I suddenly realized that this combination offered more than a way to live through tragedy and misfortune. It offered a key to a better life, through turning undesirable characteristics into positive traits. Anyone's life could be more joyful.

This lecture I was preparing would not be as helpful if I had not lived through this terrible, wrenching grief myself. I could tell my audience truthfully that crises can be growth experiences, and that we can build on what they teach us, because I had learned this the hard way. That moment of insight into the power of psychological techniques combined with the phenomenon of Reversion to the Mean started me thinking about writing this book.

## THE ANGUISH OF LONELINESS

After Milt died, I had no motivation, no energy, no nothing. I could see no future for myself. All I had was my loneliness. It seemed like a cold, black cloud. I could almost touch it.

Loneliness comes in two flavors—social and emotional. Both are bitter. Social loneliness is the wretched feeling of isolation, of not belonging. For one reason or another—perhaps you moved to another area or lost your job—you have been cut off from a group you used to belong to. You no longer have a support network. This is usually fairly simple to cure. The woman who reaches out to others can put her loneliness behind her in weeks.

Emotional loneliness is more intense. It reflects the need to be intimate with someone who loves you and who is always there for you. My private definition of love has always been someone who cares about you as much as he cares about himself. When you were a child, it was your mother. As a woman, it is usually your husband. The widow has lost this person.

I thought I would die from loneliness. I felt as if it were eating me alive. I began to research the psychological literature on loneliness, thinking that if I understood it better, I could do something about it.

I discovered I was not unique. Dr. Robert Weiss, a sociologist and one of the pioneers in loneliness research, wrote, "Loneliness that involves yearning for an emotional partner is based on a conviction that the world is barren of anyone with whom a bond of love and caring can be established. It is a symptom of a specific deficiency in human relationships, just as scurvy is a symptom of a specific nutritional deficiency." He could have been talking about me.

It is the rare woman who will live out her life without experiencing loneliness. It is as common as the head cold. Yet society treats people without an intimate other, without close friends or family, as losers. People—especially middle-aged women—who live alone, who vacation alone, who go to the movies alone are considered unwanted and unattractive. What is worse, they see themselves this way. Not because they are, but because they are treated as if they were. The widow not only has lost the man she loved and with whom she has shared her life, but she is the victim of discrimination. She is a victim of both social and emotional loneliness. Why is society so cruel? Because loneliness threatens us all. There is the uneasy feeling that "it can happen to me." And, of course, it can and does.

I was fortunate in having support networks. My mother, my daughter and her husband, my sister and her family were all there for me. I was also fortunate in that my work gave me a coast-to-coast network of people with similar professional interests.

I resumed my work schedule just days after the funeral. Left to myself, I think I might have stayed in bed with the shades drawn, alone with my grief, but that was the one thing I could not do. I had commitments and contracts for months and months ahead, and they had to be honored. I could not let people down.

I got up in the morning and got dressed and caught the plane to Chicago or Los Angeles or Phoenix, wherever I had a lecture commitment or a seminar. I got up in the morning and put on my makeup and rushed into Manhattan to do a television interview or a radio spot, or meet with the executives of one of the corporations that retain me as a consultant. I got up in the morning and dressed and wrote my column, worked on my lectures and answered the mail. And every night I went to bed and cried myself to sleep.

I had no glimmering that I was doing anything positive. I was just trying to get through day after day. But I now understand that I was doing something right. I was doing the best I could. I was Acting As If. I was Acting As If I were a woman who was involved in all facets of her professional life. In time, my Acting As If turned into the real thing. I was no longer centered on how miserable I felt. I was involved professionally and personally with others.

## REVERSION TO THE MEAN TO THE RESCUE

In the year after Milt's death, I had more serious colds, complete with coughs and sneezes and aches and fevers, than in all my years of married life. My emotional health was equally rocky. I was full of anger. I felt life had played a rotten, dirty trick on me. Every time I saw a couple walking arm-in-arm down the street, bitterness and self-pity welled up in me. They had each other, and I had no one.

So how did Reversion to the Mean help transform this self-pitying, grieving, angry and brokenhearted wreck into a functioning, joyful woman once again? Reversion to the Mean is not exactly chicken broth. It is nothing that warms and comforts you. It works silently and invisibly. It is opposed to excess, whether it is excess grief or excess joy. It is almost as if Mother Nature were saying, "There, there, you're overstressed. It's time to calm down."

One of the first hints of my return to a less self-centered state was that as the months went by, my tears for myself turned into tears for Milt who had such a love for life and for his family. I cried when I thought how he would never plant another tree in our orchard at the farm, would never set up his telescope in the field at midnight to watch the stars, would never tell another of his silly jokes.

Another move away from the depths of grief was that I began to value my time alone. One Saturday I found myself thinking, "Thank goodness I don't have to sit in front of the television and watch football all afternoon." Milt used to be glued to the set during football season, and he liked to have me there with him. Given my druthers, I would have spent those Saturday afternoons raking leaves or walking along the river. It was just a little thing, but a move in the right direction.

I began to accept that life could be good even though I was alone. Little by little, I was shaping a new life for myself without even thinking about it. I had always turned down projects that involved my spending more than one night away from home, or that meant I had to be away over a weekend, because my marriage came first and weekends were family time. Now I began to take on new projects. I was just as happy to spend the weekend in Los Angeles or Dallas as in New York. Every new offer was a Positive Reinforcement. Many of them opened up new fields for my expertise. I felt needed. I felt part of the world.

For nearly forty years, Milt had been part of me, the other half of me. Now I was beginning to be whole by myself. My life was full. Not happy. But I understood that one day it could be.

Each step away from anger and grief came as a surprise. When I realized I was getting up every morning eager to start the day . . . when I realized it had been weeks since I had cried myself to sleep . . . when I realized that I had had dinner in Los Angeles with a man I had just met and had enjoyed myself . . . when I realized how far I had come from those black days of tears and terrors, then I understood that nature is always there at our elbow, pushing us to modify those behaviors that keep us from realizing our potential for accomplishment and joy.

All one has to do is take the first step and, thanks to Reversion to the Mean, eventually everything seems to fall in place. If I had given into myself and locked myself up in the apartment to brood and grieve, I would have enjoyed none of the satisfactions and achievements of the last few years. But because, in the words of poet Robert Frost, I had "promises to keep and miles to go before I sleep," I had had to push myself out into the world and do the best I could to fulfill my commitments. And this was enough to invoke the aid of Reversion to the Mean.

If I were allowed to give only one piece of advice to a new widow, it would be: If you have a job, return to it as fast as you can. And if you do not have a job, get one. This latter is a little bit harder. You have to push yourself. As I said, if I had not had all those commitments, I might have stayed in bed and cried. Find something—either part-time or full-time, paid or volunteer—that will take you out of the house a few mornings a week. I cannot stress enough how important this is.

It gives structure to your life.
It gets you out of the house.
It gets you involved with other people.
It gives you something different to think about.
It gives you a support network.

This last item is important, because most widows discover that their social life dries up now that they are no longer part of a couple. Most people live in a Noah's Ark version of the world, where we go about two by two. The idea of an extra woman throws them. Some of your old friends will stick with you through thick and thin. Others will drift away. You have to start making a world for yourself.

## A NEW LIFE FOR A NEW WOMAN

Acting As If is not the only psychological tool to help the widow (or anyone who has suffered such a loss) regain her equilibrium. There is a solid bit of folk wisdom that advises "Make no decisions for a year." In other words, don't sell your house unless you have to; don't move to the country or the city or wherever. Don't make any major decision that involves changing your way of life until you have twelve months of living on your own under your belt.

But you can make plans, and you have the luxury of knowing you have all the time in the world to plan and replan. This involves making a Basic Diagnostic List. Actually, I recommend making two of them.

Start the first one about a month after the funeral. Sit yourself down with pencil and paper, and think about yourself and what you want. Write down your best and worst qualities and think hard about your goals. Not what you think you should do. Not what you think your husband would have wanted you to do. Your life has changed dramatically. What would you really like to do? When you are through and have completed your Master List, lock it away. You will have started a kind of yeasty ferment in your unconscious that will eventually take shape as a new way of life. It may turn out to be very similar to your past lifestyle, as mine did, or it may lead you along a completely different path.

Six months later, make a second Basic Diagnostic List. Don't refer back to the old one. Try to erase it from your mind. When you have completed your second Master List, take out the first Diagnostic List and compare the Master Lists. What changes do they reveal in your thinking about yourself and what you want out of life?

Then ask yourself the big question. "Am I satisfied with my life as it is?" If the answer is no, then consider the goals you have listed. Which is most important to you? Go for it!

## THE SIDE EFFECTS OF WIDOWHOOD

But before you do, take a good look at those worst qualities. Loss triggers the worst in most of us. As I said earlier, I was full of anger and bitterness and self-pity, and I was well aware of it. Most widows experience these disagreeable emotional side effects in addition to their loneliness. Some women are trapped by them, as these unpleasant emotions can turn into ingrained characteristics.

If you let anger take over, you will rage through life, alienating people and exhausting your energy. If you turn into a "poor little me" full of self-pity and just sit there passively, you will not only bore people, you will never try anything new, never respond to a challenge. You will become less than what you were. As for bitterness, this is pure self-indulgence, a way of blaming the world for what happened to you. Like anger, it is both alienating and debilitating. These behaviors isolate you from the world at a time when you most need all the support you can get.

If any of these self-defeating characteristics show up on your second Master List, it would be wise to get to work on them. If you take it one step at a time, you can diminish the intensity of these emotions and free up the energy they consume to use in more positive ways. The previous section on stress will help you get started.

## THE ROAD TO RECOVERY

So how does the widow, or any woman who has lost someone dear to her, get started on the road to recovery?

At the very beginning, the Rehearsal Technique of Acting As If can be immensely helpful as a way of disciplining yourself to carry on. It helps you keep a structure in your life. And, once again, the Basic Diagnostic List helps you plan for the future in a sensible and constructive way.

But the widow needs more. Positive Reinforcements are absolutely vital. Every time you lose something, you should put something good back in your life. In my case, I seem to have put more interesting work in my life, and I have also tried for the first time in my life to surround myself with friends. Between work and family, I had never had time to cultivate friendships before. Now I do, and I treasure them.

Someday there may be another wonderful man in your life. This would be the best of all Positive Reinforcements. But don't sit around waiting for him. Dr. Willard Gaylin, a psychoanalyst who has written extensively about love, advises that you "must enter new communities and new activities, not with any expectation of finding love but [so that] the energy and force of loving can be used to exercise its restorative magic on the user." This advice applies to every widow, whether or not she hopes to remarry, for very few widows, less than 10 percent who are over forty-five when they are widowed, remarry. Widows need all the "restorative magic" they can get.

## THE PROMISE

Is it worth all this effort? It certainly is. I went through all the shock and grief and mourning, the self-doubts and self-pity, the anxieties and anger and bitterness, and I can tell you that they do come to an end. It takes two to three years for most people. And then, almost without your knowing it, life is good again. One morning when you are brushing your teeth, you look in the mirror and realize that you have not been lonely all week. In time the loneliness almost disappears.

You are left with fleeting, poignant moments when you think of how it was, and how you loved him. The tears come to your eyes, but they are tears of love. Not the tears of sorrow and self-pity and rage. You reach the point where you understand that no matter what happens in your life, his love is part of you. That knowledge will always be with you and give you strength for whatever you choose to do in this next chapter of your life.

# Chapter Twenty-two

# DIVORCE

## Not an End, a Beginning

FOR BETTER OR worse, once a woman marries, there is a 50 percent chance that divorce is in her future. And when it occurs, if one is to believe recent research, she finds it no big deal. Way back when, divorce used to be a disgrace and a scandal, but no longer. Divorce has become a commonplace.

Recent surveys of divorcées over forty found that most of them looked upon their divorce as an opportunity for growth and change. Woman after woman reported that she became stronger, had more self-esteem, was more competent and much happier after the divorce. On the whole, they looked back on their marriages as constricting and demanding. Seventy-eight percent of divorced women claimed that they were happier after the divorce. They were not particularly interested in giving marriage another chance. Many women reported enjoyable relationships with men, however, which they tended to confine to weekends. Sex, it seems, is not worth the sacrifice of freedom that marriage entails. Divorced men, on the contrary, are almost uniformly anxious to remarry.

"Women's lack of interest in marriage is the real revolution of the past twenty years," says Frances Goldscheider, professor of sociology at Brown University. "Women," she says, "no longer define themselves around men." After divorce, ". . . unlike men, they do well socially because they have friends and bonding skills."

Today's divorcée finds a new world out there that offers her a second chance at life. I won't go so far as to say that divorce is good for you, but it seems clear that it is for a great many women.

## DEEP-CRISIS TIME

If divorce is the Open Sesame to independence and self-esteem, why am I treating it as a crisis?

Because it is. The divorce itself is a matter of minutes, but the recovery may take years. The longer the marriage, the longer the recovery takes in most cases. In any case, the first six to twelve months is deep-crisis time. The foundation that a woman once thought rock-solid has shifted under her feet. Treacherous chasms open. The landscape changes. Divorce is an emotional earthquake.

Her future may be brighter, and there may be more avenues open to her, but today's divorcée suffers from the same low self-esteem, loneliness, bitterness and anxieties as her predecessors way back when divorce was disgrace.

How could it be otherwise? A good marriage is wonderful, and most marriages start out that way. There is love and support, excitement and romance, mutual growth. But there comes a time when half of these unions suffer what Shakespeare called a "sea change" that transforms the relationship into a fossil, a dead image of itself. The life has gone out of it. Mourning for what used to be is added to all the other distressing emotions that accompany divorce.

No one can tell the new divorcée what to do. She has to make her own decisions and mistakes. What I want to do in this chapter is help the divorcée understand and manage her reactions to her emotional pain and stress so that they do not become self-destructive. I also want to encourage her to get on with the rest of her life and make the most of the opportunities her divorce opens up. The postdivorce era is an opportunity for unrestricted personal growth, a fresh exploration of goals and potential.

## SIT TIGHT FOR A YEAR

The two rock-solid certainties in the deep-crisis postdivorce months are:

1. Life will be difficult.
2. You will make mistakes.

Every divorced woman makes mistakes. They are par for the course, but mistakes are not fatal. The divorcée must guard against allowing the inevitable mistakes she will make lessen her already shaky self-confidence. Mistakes are to learn from. Most postdivorce mistakes are the result of impulsiveness. This can be a charming trait at the proper time, but one that is self-defeating in the weeks and months after divorce.

The most common mistake divorcées make is to initiate an immediate and drastic change in their lives. Deep-crisis time is a time to sit tight, but too many newly divorced women intensify the emotional earthquake by making changes that add to their already heavy load of negative stress.

This is understandable. The divorcée is trying to get herself back into emotional stasis. She is miserable. Her life is empty. All she wants is to feel better and do something to fill that void in her life, so she acts. She usually decides to move. Sometimes the move is forced on her, but most of the time it is the result of an almost irresistible urge to change her environment.

Mildred learned about the false promise of impulsive decisions the hard way. After her divorce at age forty-six, she felt she had to leave the condominium apartment where she and her husband had lived, even though it was part of her divorce settlement. She did not want to live in the same city as her former husband, let alone the same apartment.

She sold the apartment and moved from Manhattan to a New Jersey suburb, a typical bedroom community. She was confident that she had thought through all the pros and cons. The house was in good condition, the rent reasonable and it was an easy commute to her paralegal job in the city.

At first she was busy getting settled and finding her way around. But as time went by, loneliness set in. When she got home after work, she felt marooned.

"I'd walk around the neighborhood after supper and people would be out watering their lawns, shooting baskets with their kids, sitting on the porch chatting. But nobody said hello, nobody waved. It was as if I was invisible.

"I went to a couple of public meetings that were advertised in the local paper—one about the town budget, the other about installing a traffic light in front of the supermarket. No one spoke to me. I was the woman who was not there. The loneliest woman in town."

Mildred had never considered the fact that a divorced woman—actually any single woman—may have a hard time establishing herself in a family-oriented suburb. Especially a woman who worked in the city five days a week.

After some desperately lonely months, she rethought her situation. All her friends lived in the city. By moving to the suburbs, she had cut herself off from the casual after-five socializing she was used to. After the divorce, she had promised herself that she would lead a full and stimulating life, but instead she had neatly defeated herself. "I felt as if I had lost a year out of my life. It was as if I had sentenced myself to a jail term in an isolation cell," she told me.

She had made a mistake. But she did not have to live with it forever. When her lease was up, she moved back to Manhattan, with a better idea of the kind of life she wanted.

When Mildred told me her story several years later, I sighed. I wished I had known her at the time of her divorce. I would have suggested that she use two of my psychological tools before making any change in her life. The Basic Diagnostic List and the Worst-Case Scenario would have helped her control her impulsiveness and kept her from making such a drastic change.

The Diagnostic List would have forced her to think about what she wanted from the new life that her divorce had opened up. And a Worst-Case Scenario, outlining the worst possible outcomes if she moved to the suburbs or if she stayed in the city, would almost certainly have prevented her from making that unfortunate move. Using these two psychological techniques, she would have realized that it was most unlikely that in a city of some eight million people she would ever run into her former husband. She would also have thought twice about moving away from old friends, especially when the move was a matter of whim, rather than necessity.

We learn from our mistakes, though. Mildred learned that she had cherished a mistakenly romantic picture of suburban life, something on the order of living in an idyllic village where everyone knew everyone. She also learned how much her friends meant to her, and how much she enjoyed city life.

The best single piece of advice I can give a divorcée is the same I give widows: Sit tight for a year. I know how hard it is to follow this advice, but try. For a year, don't make any change that is not absolutely necessary. Don't sell your house. Don't move in with your daughter. Don't remarry. Don't buy a condo in Mexico or a cabin in Alaska. Don't buy that stock. Don't make that loan. And for heaven's sake, don't go to bed with that man you just met (how do you know he does not have AIDS?). Put everything on hold for twelve months. When you are in the middle of an emotional earthquake, you can't always tell which way is up. So, protect yourself.

You are not only at emotional sixes and sevens, you are probably not in great physical shape. Divorce and illness go together just the way love and marriage are supposed to. During the first year, that deep-crisis time, divorcées are ill more often and more seriously than married women of the same age. Loneliness and shattered self-esteem, those almost inevitable companions of divorce, seem to weaken the immune system. The divorcée is also more prone to injuries from stumbles, falls, automobile accidents, burns and so on.

Keep these vulnerabilities in mind and don't make lifestyle changes during this period. You are already coping with a major change. Don't add to your negative stress load. Take care of yourself.

## ANTIDOTES FOR ALIENATING EMOTIONS

Bitterness and self-pity are part and parcel of the emotional baggage of divorce. They are perfectly natural reactions, but they are also destructive and unattractive. If you let yourself wallow in them, they will trash the new life you are trying to build for yourself. You want to emerge from the trauma of divorce as a victor, not a victim.

No one wants to be around a woman who is forever talking about the raw deal she got, and how that rat and his slick lawyer got away with murder and how she would like to see them fry in hell. Most people are initially sympathetic, but their tolerance wears thin when the divorcée keeps moaning about her sorry lot and carrying on about how no one ever had it so bad.

Instead of rehashing the past, the divorcée should be looking ahead. She should be trying to build a new support network or bolster her old one, since a woman usually emerges from divorce minus most of the marital circle of friends. If her bitterness and self-pity keep spilling over, she will alienate the friends who have stuck with her as well as any new acquaintances she makes.

The way to control these unpleasant behaviors is to confront them, understand them, defang them and then get along with one's life. Two psychological tools that divorced women have found helpful are Negative Reinforcement and Acting As If.

Connie used her own personal version of the Negative Reinforcement List to curtail her bitterness. As I pointed out earlier, all the psychological techniques I outline in this book can be adapted to fit almost any individual situation or need. Connie called her version the Antidote List.

Every time she had a bitter thought about her former husband or said something derogatory about him, she forced herself to write something good about him in her little notebook. One night, for instance, when she couldn't fall asleep, she started stewing about his duplicity.

"What a bastard David was," she thought indignantly. "Always talking about how tight money was, and all the time he was spending thousands on that woman, buying her a pre-engagement ring and a fur coat while he was telling me we couldn't afford to buy a new refrigerator." When she realized she was giving in to bitterness, she scrambled out of bed, grabbed her notebook and wrote an antidote. "He was really nice that time I totaled the new car. All he said was 'Accidents happen. That's why we have insurance.' Some men would have been furious." If she caught herself running him down to a friend, she would pull out the notebook and jot down a few words to remind her to provide a positive antidote later when she was alone.

The list helped Connie gain a better perspective on her former husband. She realized that like everyone else, David was a mixture of good and bad. He was not the Galahad she had thought him when they were first married, nor was he the villain that she had thought him when he said he wanted a divorce. And now he was out of her life.

Her Antidote List had not only suppressed her bitter thoughts and comments about her ex-husband, but had rooted out the bitterness. By counteracting her resentment and anger with examples of his good points, she was able to dilute her bitter feelings.

"As I kept on with it, I discovered that I became less and less bitter," she reported. "In fact, I got so bored thinking about him that I've been able to put him out of my thoughts and out of my life." This was a case of a psychological technique and the law of Reversion to the Mean working in perfect synchronization to modify a self-destructive reaction.

Acting As If is another useful antidote for bitterness. Janet's divorce had been painful. She had been deeply shaken to think that her husband of seventeen years could be as cruelly vindictive as he showed himself to be during their divorce proceedings. However, in public, she made a point of Acting As If. She Acted As If everything had gone smoothly and as if she had no bad feelings, just regret that they had not been able to make the marriage work. As far as the world was concerned, she had no bitterness, no self-pity, no criticisms.

"I started Acting As If out of pride," Janet said. "I couldn't bear to let people know how badly I had been treated. After a while, I found that I really didn't care. So what if he had acted like a beast? It was all over and done with.

"I have always been glad that I did not let anyone know how bitterly angry and sorry for myself I was. All it would have done would be to make me feel worse.

"Feeling good about yourself," she concluded, "is the best cure there is for bitterness and self-pity."

## ESTABLISHING ONE'S OWN IDENTITY

At bottom, divorce is about loss. You lose a marriage, a lifestyle, even your identity. You were Mrs. John Jones. No longer. There may even be a new Mrs. John Jones. Now you are Jane Jones, divorcée. (Or did you take back your maiden name? This has certain advantages when it comes to establishing your new identity. It gets you out of the shadow of the past.) But who is Jane? Not even Jane knows at this point.

Whether he wanted out or she wanted out, the divorcée usually feels emotionally steamrollered and may consider herself a reject, a discard. She is fortunate if she walks away from the divorce with even the remnants of her former support network. But she does gain something—the chance to establish her own identity as an individual, to be the real Jane. It may be the first time in her adult life that she has been able to consider her own wishes without reference to anyone else's, the first chance she has had in a long, long time to put herself first.

This is a time to bet on yourself and on the future, to find the real you. You are never going to depart from your basic personality, the inner core that you were born with, but you can become more outgoing, more thoughtful, more fun-loving, less rigid, less timorous, less aggressive. You can move in a new direction and build a more satisfying life for yourself. You can become the person you have the potential to be.

Finding and establishing this new identity cannot be done overnight. Don't expect to emerge from the chrysalis of your old identity in a matter of days or weeks. It is a matter of one small step at a time, of finding out what feels right. And it is never too soon to start. This is your great chance to get whatever you want out of life. It is the silver lining to the storm cloud of divorce.

First of all, you have to rebuild that shaky self-esteem. Nothing is going to feel right until you feel good about yourself. Even a woman who initiates the divorce develops a self-esteem deficit. She wakes up in the middle of the night and thinks she should have tried harder to make the marriage work, or perhaps it was a mistake or the problems in the marriage had all been her fault. Worse, there is no one there to tell her she's being silly and she should go back to sleep and she'll feel better in the morning.

This is a time to polish up your self-image. How do you look? After what you have been through, you may need a little sprucing up. Yes, this is purely superficial, but appearance is important—for your own self-confidence and for your Halo Effect. A positive Halo Effect generates self-confidence as you respond to the favorable way others respond to you. Look at yourself with a cold eye. How about the hair, the makeup, the figure, the wardrobe? Do you need to repackage yourself?

Some women have to learn to invest in themselves, to spend money on their appearance. If as a wife or mother you tended to put everyone else's needs first, you need to learn that it's your time now. This may mean putting yourself in the hands of a good hairdresser or taking advantage of the free makeovers offered at many cosmetic counters in department stores. You don't have to buy anything unless it makes you look wonderful. Then get yourself at least one complete new outfit that really does something for you. Your new look is the beginning of your new identity.

## THE TOOLS FOR THE JOB

The next step is to reach into your Psychological Tool Kit and pull out the tools you need to find out who you are and what you want. This is a major project and you will need tools from every category:

- A Positive Reinforcement List
- A Basic Diagnostic List
- A Condensed Diagnostic List
- Both Positive and Negative Reinforcement
- A Worst-Case Scenario
- Previsualization

If you start using these psychological techniques today, you will feel a lot better about yourself in six weeks. You may even have established a new direction for your life.

To begin with, start work on your Basic Diagnostic List and a Positive Reinforcement List. The Reinforcement List should start paying off in a week or ten days. The Diagnostic List is longterm therapy.

The Reinforcement List is directed at boosting your self-esteem. It is simple and good for the soul. Every night before you go to bed, write down in a little notebook everything you did that day that was kind or helpful or admirable or special, everything that made you feel good about yourself. If you had any compliments, write each one of them down. Don't go to bed without writing at least three good things about yourself. Even if you have had a rotten day, you can at least note that you make scrambled eggs better than anyone else you know or that you are getting good at applying your new eyeliner. You don't have to rescue someone from drowning or win the Nobel Prize every day.

The sneaky psychological twist to this kind of Reinforcement List is that you start doing things that make you feel good about yourself because you want to have something to write down. Believe me, if you keep this up, your self-esteem will go up, too.

The most important aid in your search for the real you is that old reliable, the Basic Diagnostic List. It will give you a start on a master plan for making the most of yourself. Spend time on it, especially on thinking about your goals. You have a whole new life ahead of you. What do you want to do? What do you want to achieve?

By the end of the month, when you have completed the Master List, you should have a good idea of your immediate goal. Since it may change from time to time as you become more confident of your abilities, it is a good idea to make the Basic Diagnostic List an annual event to find out whether you are still on the right track or if your goal has changed.

Use the Condensed Diagnostic List to evaluate the feasibility of your goal and whether it is compatible with your personality. Do this a week or two after you have analyzed your Basic Diagnostic Master List. You may discover that you have one or two behaviors that might stand in the way of your achieving that goal, but you are now familiar with the Operant Conditioning techniques that can help modify these self-defeating traits and strengthen your good qualities.

Follow up the Condensed Diagnostic List with a Worst-Case

Scenario—the worst that could happen if you go for whatever it is, and the worst that could happen if you don't.

At this point, you are ready to start Previsualizing. Previsualization offers a way to think yourself through a new role or lifestyle, to see yourself taking the kind of actions that are necessary to attain it, to rehearse everything before doing anything. I suggest having a Previsualization session once a week. This can do wonders for your self-confidence. Settle yourself quietly and comfortably and Previsualize what you want your life to be. See yourself leading that life, competently and happily. See yourself full of confidence, among friends, proud of yourself because you have remade your life. It can all come true.

Just one last word. Remember that basic rule about sitting tight for a year. Don't feel that you must rush into anything—especially if it involves a change in lifestyle. These psychological techniques take time, but their effects escalate over the weeks and months. Even when you have settled on a goal that feels right, you do not have to rush off and save the rain forests or start law school or open that catering service tomorrow. Give yourself that important year of grace to think about what you want and need.

# Chapter Twenty-three

# GETTING FIRED

---

## And Regaining Self-Esteem

---

JOB LOSS ON a major scale has escalated to crisis proportions in the first half of this decade. Megacorporations have "downsized" and small businesses have gone to the wall. The axe has fallen on white- and blue-collar workers, junior and senior executives, clerks and laborers alike. It is taking white-collar workers more and more time to find a new position—an average minimum of seven months—and nearly half of the present unemployed will have to settle for positions paying less than those they lost.

Being fired, especially when it is through no fault of your own, knocks you right off your emotional and financial feet. You feel worthless, angry, disoriented and, once the shock wears off, insecure and fearful. You are up in the air. What do you do?

You should not do anything for at least a week or two if you are looking for something above entry-level. Any job-seeking approaches you make will almost certainly be self-defeating until you have recovered from the shock and can think clearly about what you should do.

You can, however, start pushing yourself back to emotional normalcy. Even if you feel the bottom of the world has fallen out, that law of Reversion to the Mean can help you get back to emotional equilibrium if you take the first step. One way to do this is to get to work with your Psychological Tool Kit.

## THE SILVER LINING

Some people ask, "Why me?" as if fate has it in for them. It just might be that fate is on your side. There is always a silver lining to adversity, although sometimes you have to look awfully hard to find it. The silver lining here is that you are forced to examine what you can do and what you want to do, to weigh your strengths and your weaknesses, to set new goals for yourself.

There are not many luxuries in being unemployed, but the luxury of contemplating your life and your future has been forced on you and you should take advantage of the opportunity. An excellent way to do this is to make out a Basic Diagnostic List. In this situation, I suggest making two versions. The first is the standard Diagnostic List of your good and bad qualities and your goals. The second is a variation, a diagnosis of your former job along the following lines. Follow the same procedures and observe the same time frame as for the Basic Diagnostic List.

| Its Assets | Its Drawbacks | Its Future |
|---|---|---|
| 1. | 1. | 1. |
| 2. | 2. | 2. |
| 3. | 3. | 3. |

You may be impatient and protest that "I can't spend weeks working on lists. I've got to start looking for a job." The answers to this are "Yes, you can" and "No, you don't."

When you have analyzed your Job Diagnosis and Self-Diagnostic Master Lists, you can start thinking constructively. More than that, you can now think on two levels. First, how to attain your immediate goal, a job. And second, how to attain your ultimate goal, what you really want to do with your life.

When you have completed the Master List for your job diagnosis, you will have a good idea of how good a fit your previous job was for your skills and personality. You may see that it was a mismatch, a career detour. Or you may decide that, on the whole, you and the job were a good match, but you were not being used to your full capacity, and you were ready to move up a couple of notches.

Your Self-Diagnostic Master List will give you insight into what you really want. You may find that your strongest qualities were of little importance in your former job. Or that the qualities you see as your worst could be assets in a different line of work.

You are at a turning point in your life. Should you turn right or left? Or continue straight ahead? It may be that you can turn this career setback into a leap forward or even sideways. This may be a blessed opportunity to change direction, something you would never have risked doing when you had a good-paying position. But now you have nothing to lose. A change of direction might just be the start of a better life.

You will probably be surprised at what you learn about yourself and what you want to do. After you spend some time analyzing these two Master Lists, you will know more about yourself, your priorities and your goals, and you can look for a job, knowing what it is you want.

## CLEARING AWAY THE UNDERBRUSH

Before you start a job hunt, it is important to get under control the self-defeating stresses triggered by dismissal. You can't sell yourself to anyone if you feel like a busted balloon, are rigid with fear or consumed by anger.

Don't make the mistake of trying to suppress these emotions.

It would be surprising if you were not angry and full of anxiety, if your self-esteem were not in the cellar. Some people think that if they face these emotions, they may fall apart, so they whistle a merry tune and try to kid themselves that everything is fine. The act wears thin in a short time, and the stress is all the greater for having been denied.

The longer you have been with a company, the more angry you are likely to be about being let go. Men and women in their fifties who have been with a company for years and years tend to be angriest. While there has never been anything in writing, they often feel as if it was understood that, after all these years, they had attained job security. Now their unwritten contract has not been honored, and they are outraged.

Your anger may be understandable, even justified, but it is self-defeating. I recommend using the techniques explained in Chapter Nineteen to dissipate it so that you will be neither a Hoarder nor an Exploder.

The best way to rid yourself of this kind of dead-end anger on a short-term basis is to use Negative Reinforcement. When the anger wells up, drop everything and go for a long, fast walk, work out at the gym or wax the floors. The harder you exercise, the more you will increase the production of those endorphins that give you a more benign outlook on the world. This will give you a temporary respite and allow you to distance yourself from your anger.

You are under enough stress as it is without having to cope with the stress produced by anger. Anger can be self-defeating when you interview for a new position. Skilled interviewers probe for anger and grudge-holding, especially with a job applicant who has been laid off. No one wants to hire a potential sorehead.

Your anxieties, on the other hand, are based on reality, although they may often be exaggerated simply because you feel so insecure. You worry about how long you will be able to pay the rent or the mortgage. How long it will take to get a new job.

Will you end up having to live with friends? These are valid concerns, but you must not let them get out of hand. Making out the two Basic Diagnostic Lists will help calm your worries, simply because you are doing something constructive about your situation.

When I lecture about anxiety, one of the coping techniques I recommend to my audiences is to write down whatever is worrying them. Research has shown that this is a very effective way to dissipate anxieties. In one study of a group of professionals who had lost their jobs, half of them were asked to write about the trauma caused by their job loss. They were told to write down every anxiety that came into their heads—how they had reacted to being fired, their financial and other worries, the effect on their sleeping habits and sex life, their relationships with family and friends. The other half of the group of unemployed professionals served as controls, writing nothing.

The group who wrote about their anxieties reported that they felt better afterward. But the most striking finding was that more than half of that group found new positions in eight months, while only 14 percent of those who had not been asked to write about their anxieties had found employment.

One of the directors of the study, Dr. James Pennebaker of Southern Methodist University in Dallas, has discovered that writing about one's anxieties is helpful in many situations such as divorce, financial difficulties, problems with one's children or spouse. People tend to feel better about themselves and more confident after getting their anxieties down on paper.

The single best antidote for fears about the future is a Worst-Case Scenario. I outlined a variation in Chapter Eighteen for the person who fears she might lose her job. If you have actually lost your job, use the same format but change the headings to:

WHY DID I LOSE MY JOB?
THE WORST THAT COULD HAPPEN
WHAT I WOULD DO IF IT DID

### What Should I Do Now?
### What Do I Want to Do?

Make as many entries under each heading as you can, and be as specific as possible about each entry. You may find that there are options you had not considered. At the very least, you will have organized your thoughts and written down specific actions that you plan to take. You will find that having a master plan that deals with your fears and outlines the positive steps you plan to take to change your situation will minimize your anxieties.

Once you have brought your anger and anxieties a little closer to the norm, they will not get in the way of your job hunt and your future. Of course you will still be angry and full of worries, but this is normal for a person who has lost her job. All you need to do is get those emotions under control, so that you can plan and act on the basis of cool logic.

## PUTTING YOUR LIFE BACK TOGETHER

Until very recently, practically no research was done on the effect of job loss on women. It was thought that women were not as traumatized by job loss as men, partly because their identities were less dependent upon their work.

If this was ever true, it is no longer. A recent study reveals that a woman's reaction to job loss is different from a man's. Most men begin their search for a new job almost immediately, while most women tend to put it off for a couple of weeks or even longer. Women's first reaction is to turn to friends and family for emotional support. Then, once they feel somewhat stabilized, they start job hunting. The researchers speculated that this indicated women were more traumatized by job loss than men. This may be, but one could make a case that both sexes are equally traumatized by job loss, and that women simply handle their stress more wisely. They give themselves a breathing period to get over the shock and plan what they will do.

Most people who have lost their jobs have to go through a mourning period for all that they have lost. It is not just the loss of the job and the salary that makes you feel so insecure and uncertain, it is the loss of a way of life. This seems to be experienced equally strongly by both sexes.

For most people, their office is another home, their colleagues another family. You lunch with them, gripe with them, compete with them. You discuss what kind of car Sheila should buy and reassure Sam that his bald spot is not all that noticeable. You know about their family problems. When you had the miscarriage or the gall-bladder problem, they were there for you. Now this home and that family have been broken up, overnight. You may go back to visit, but you no longer belong there. That little world is spinning along without you. You have lost what was probably your most important social network outside of your own family.

This has to be replaced. If your job search stretches into months—and these days this is the rule, not the exception—it is important to reach out for people and reconstruct your social network.

Volunteering is a wonderful way to pull more people into your life and at the same time help your job search. Give some thought to the organization you choose to help. Ideally it should offer you an opportunity to make useful contacts.

Diana volunteered to help with her local hospital's fund-raising drive. This involved meetings with hospital administrators and physicians who explained where and how the money would be used, as well as with the other volunteers as they worked out their schedules and duties. Most of the fund-raising volunteers were solid citizens, many of them with important positions.

Diana made a point of letting people know she was looking for a job in public relations. She also made a point of working her head off at fund-raising. She still had plenty of time for job hunting and interviews, but her new job came through one of her new fund-raising acquaintances who called to tell her that he had heard of an opening that might interest her.

She not only found exactly the kind of job she wanted, but she had made several good friends and provided herself with an effective and useful support network to replace the one she had lost.

Volunteer activities also look great on a resumé. They show that you did more than just sit around at home. Another way to get a support network is to work part-time. It is fairly easy to find part-time positions if you are willing to work evenings or weekends, and this leaves your days free for job hunting, too.

## PUMPING UP YOUR SELF-ESTEEM

A loss of self-esteem almost inevitably goes along with the loss of a job, although it should not. The person who has lost her job knows that she has been doing a good job, that through the years she has received raises and promotions and that the only reason she was fired was that business was bad, but she still feels as if somehow it was her fault.

The unemployed woman often blames herself. It is easier to blame oneself than a bad economy or bad management. It is important for you to understand that there are times when factors beyond your control are at work. If it was not your fault, then there is no reason for you to lose confidence in yourself. However, even if you are convinced of this intellectually, it may be hard to convince yourself emotionally.

You have suffered a double blow to your self-esteem. You feel worthless—first, because you don't have a job; and second, because you have lost your identity. Or think that you have. In our society, people tend to define themselves by their jobs. Bill is a CPA. Sally is an account executive. Alex is a corporate librarian. Adele is a systems analyst. But when you have lost your job, what are you? You are unemployed. You feel humiliated. You are a reject, a failure. This is nonsense, of course, but it is the way many people feel.

The best way to get back to feeling good about yourself, and seeing things as they really are and not as your anxieties paint them, is to Act As If. First of all, Act As If you still had a job. In a way, you do. Your job is to find a new job. Get up every morning and dress and groom as if you were going to the office. You have appointments to make, appointments to keep. And if interviews are few and far between, get yourself a volunteer job the way Diana did. Keep yourself busy eight hours a day. As you go through the day, Act As If you are confident, interested in the process of finding a new spot for yourself, involved in what is going on in the world.

You want to establish a Positive Halo Effect. This may be the most effective asset anyone can bring to a job interview. When you meet people for the first time, you want them to see you as an attractive, well-groomed person who is busy and committed, a hard worker. It may be hard at first to give this impression when you are feeling like a reject, but if you Act As If, people will see you as the person you project. And very soon, you will see yourself the same way—as someone with a lot to offer. This is what happened to Esther.

Esther described herself as shell-shocked. "I had identified myself with my job selling advertising space for a monthly magazine. Part of my world collapsed when they told me they were doing away with the whole department and turning it over to an outside agency to save on salaries and benefits."

She went into a funk for a couple of weeks. She stayed in bed until noon, let the telephone ring until whoever it was gave up, spent most of the time reading romance novels and watching television. Her husband was about to insist that she get some counseling, when she snapped out of it. She looked at herself in the bathroom mirror one morning and was horrified. "I looked like a witch. My hair was a mess. I looked like something that lived under a rock."

The shock was enough to get her up and out. "I wasn't going

to let people say that I had fallen apart and looked like the devil." She treated herself to a facial and a new hairstyle, and went home and cooked dinner for the first time in two weeks.

She got on the telephone and called everyone she knew. "I'm back in town," she announced. "Let's have lunch. I want to catch up on the gossip." In no time at all, her calendar was full for weeks ahead. She did not think of it as Acting As If, but that is exactly what she was doing. She was determined not to let anyone know how badly she had been rocked by losing her job. When people asked where she had been, she parried the question. "Nowhere interesting," she would say. "I just wanted to get away for a few days." Everyone told her she looked great. "I had a good rest," she would reply. Actually, a short vacation is often a good idea if it is within your budget. The change of environment gives you a better perspective on your situation.

A few weeks later, Esther and her husband gave a cocktail party. She was still Acting As If, Acting As If everything was coming up roses. "What are you going to do? Have you any plans?" one of the guests asked.

Without even thinking, Esther said, "I'm going into business for myself. Providing advertising services for small businesses." The minute she said this, she knew it was exactly what she wanted to do, although it had been a purely spontaneous reply to the question.

Sometimes we honestly do not know what we feel deep down. This is why the Basic Diagnostic List is so valuable. It helps you get at subconscious feelings and goals. Esther's blue funk may have been responsible for this sudden insight. She may have retreated from the world, but her subconscious had kept on working.

That night after everyone had gone home, she and her husband talked it over. "I've got the skills and the contacts," she said, "but it's a real gamble."

"There's nothing wrong with taking a chance," he said, "as long as you know when to cut your losses. Why don't you give it a try? If you haven't gotten anywhere in a year, then drop it."

They decided she could work from home at the beginning, which would keep expenses at a minimum. Esther spent three months researching her market, then announced the opening of a new agency, which would serve small businesses and shops in the New York suburbs. She started with one client, a friend who had a small dress shop specializing in top-of-the-line fashions.

Esther designed and wrote ads for the shop and placed them in the appropriate media. In two months, her friend's sales had nearly doubled. With this success under her belt, Esther was able to assemble a group of small accounts. By the end of the year, her agency was paying its own way. It was on the verge of making a profit. She was fortunate in that everything fell into place for her. She had the skills, the energy and was able to keep on going for the year and a half it took for her business to start turning a profit.

When she thought back to the humiliating funk and panic she had experienced when she was fired, she could hardly believe it. Acting As If gives that little nudge to the phenomenon of Reversion to the Mean that helps restore your self-esteem. And there is usually a bonus. When you have gone through a crisis and survived, you emerge as a stronger person.

But sometimes in the middle of a crisis, it is hard to believe that things will ever get any better. And when this happens, give yourself some Positive Reinforcement with Previsualization of how things are going to be. See yourself having a job interview that goes well, being offered the new position and handling it superbly. Previsualization is not wishful thinking, it is constructive thinking. It helps you look ahead, see how things might be, and gives you specific goals to work toward.

It gives you the expectation of success. This is the most positive and powerful reaction to job-loss stress there is—short of a new job. It will keep you thinking you will succeed, trying to succeed, working toward the goal. It will keep you from giving up. Expectation of success is the most powerful magnet in attracting success.

I wish I could promise you that these psychological techniques will get you a new job. But in these years of downsizing, with hundreds of thousands of people looking for work, this is impossible. What I can promise you is that they will give you an edge over other job-seekers. They will help you modify any self-defeating traits. They will help you think clearly and boost your self-esteem. They will give you a positive attitude, a feeling that you can handle whatever roadblock life has put in your way, and you can.

*Chapter Twenty-four*

# THE LAST CHAPTER

---

## How to Live Young

---

NOT ALL CRISES are terrible life-rending happenings. Some are turning points, times when you face the inevitable. Like age, for instance. Aging may be accompanied by disabilities or circumstances that must be faced in much the same way one has to face the loss of a job or a marriage or a husband. The loss of youth is part of the continuum of life. There is no getting away from the knowledge that our lives will end one day. And there is no reason why the last chapter of the continuum should be any less rewarding than those that have gone before.

Chronological age is nothing but a record of how many years you have lived. Biological age and mental age are what really count. They govern your health, your energy, your zest, your delight in life. Everyone knows the fifty-year-old who is full of creaks and complaints, and the eighty-year-old who is full of energy and open to new ideas and experiences. Scientists have proved that it is perfectly possible to turn back the clock on biological and mental age. You will never be thirty again, but you can have the thirty-year-old's open mind. You can live young, and if you do, you will probably live longer. One's true age is more a matter of attitude than of years.

## WHEN IS OLD AGE?

When do we start thinking of ourselves as old? Women used to consider menopause the beginning of old age. Today we think of it as a new beginning and a new freedom. For some the onset of age comes with retirement. Or a certain birthday, or when you realize you are outliving many of your peers. It may be after an illness or an accident that forced a change in lifestyle.

Many people seem to cross the line that divides the prime of life from old age after a severe stress or life-crisis. This is understandable, but it is also undesirable and unnecessary. If your descent into feeling old is a consequence of such stress, you have become a victim of a self-defeating attitude. Nobody ever promised us a smooth ride through life. As I have explained, the stress-free life is not worth living unless you always wanted to be a vegetable. Stress develops strength and can be turned into an asset, a source of energy, at any age. And this energy can be used to turn back the biological and brain clocks.

## TURNING BACK THE BIOLOGICAL CLOCK

Turning back one's biological clock does not mean turning back the clock of years. Nothing can be done about that relentless progression. It means turning back your body clock to regain health and energy. Dr. William J. Evans of the Human Nutrition Research Center on Aging at Tufts University is one of the researchers who have established that it is quite possible to be younger than one's chronological age.

"No matter what your present health," Dr. Evans says, "regular exercise and improved eating habits will lower your biological age." His prescription for a younger body is simple—increase muscle mass and decrease body fat by exercise and diet.

This sounds too dull to be true. It is the kind of thing your mother used to tell you—drink your milk and eat your veggies. But it works. Other scientists have corroborated his findings.

One of them, Dr. Lester Breslow of the University of California, has been following the lives of 7,000 Californians for nearly thirty years. He chose the participants in his study because they were leading healthy lives. It turned out that they shared five characteristics:

1. They used alcohol very moderately.
2. They did not smoke.
3. They kept their weight down.
4. They got seven to eight hours sleep a night.
5. They exercised regularly.

His major finding at the twenty-eight-year point of the study was that these men and women who had observed the same kind of healthy lifestyle that Dr. Evans recommends were as physically fit as a control group of people thirty years younger than they were! The control group had not followed such a healthy regime.

Neither Dr. Evans nor Dr. Breslow recommend anything expensive or exotic like injections or miracle potions. You have heard or read about the benefits of low-fat diets and exercise for years and years. The news is that time has shown that they work, and that it is never too late to start. Women in their nineties have gained strength and energy when they followed this prescription for turning back the biological clock.

## STICKING TO THE NEW LIFESTYLE

If exercise and a low-fat diet, moderate use of alcohol and abstaining from smoking can turn back your biological clock five, ten, twenty or more years, it certainly seems worth the effort. It may be hard to stick to this regime if you have been a bit lazy physically and a bit overindulgent at the dinner table. It is all too easy to decide that you will have the whipped-cream special just this once, or to tell yourself you are too busy to exercise today.

You can use Positive Reinforcement and the Rehearsal Techniques to make it easier for you to stay with the program and turn back the clock. Keeping a Positive Reinforcement List will help maintain this healthy way of life until it becomes a habit. Write down what kind of exercise you did each day and how long you did it, and note what you ate at each meal. If you skimped on exercise or overdid it on fat intake, write down the reason why. If possible, jot down ways to prevent this in the future. Go over your entries once a week and evaluate your progress. It takes time to establish new habits, especially when you are tackling two at the same time, so I recommend maintaining the Reinforcement List for at least three or four months.

I also recommend consulting your doctor before you start and asking him what exercises you should do. Ideally, there should be a mix of aerobic exercise and weight-lifting to increase muscle mass and strength. Your physician can prescribe the kind of exercise, how often you should do it and the weight of your weights.

Previsualization is another way to establish new habits. Take fifteen minutes a day to relax and Previsualize yourself as you will be—stronger, more energetic, feeling younger. Visualize that body clock turning backward instead of forward. Visualize yourself as making constant progress. This kind of Previsualization makes what you are doing seem more real. You will expect yourself to behave in the ways you Previsualize.

Once you have started on this new regime, you will be subtracting weeks and months and eventually years from your biological age, with the result that your body will serve you better and longer.

## TURNING BACK THE MENTAL CLOCK

Even more important than turning back the biological clock is turning back the mental clock. It is the mind that governs our actions. Turning back its clock demands a positive attitude, a can-do approach to life rather than a can't-do or can't-be-bothered-to-do approach.

I have a friend who looks to be in her late fifties or early sixties, but is actually in her mid-seventies. Her secret? She watches her diet, walks two miles a day and stays busy, busy, busy. She Acts As If she were young and so she is perceived that way.

She has a part-time job as a receptionist in a doctor's office. She also works three nights a week as a literacy volunteer helping foreign-born women to read and write English. Twice a month she invites five people—old friends, new acquaintances, friends of friends, new people in town—to her apartment for Sunday-night supper. The food is always simple, a casserole or a salad, depending on the season, but the talk is animated.

"I always try to have someone the others don't know," she told me. "That makes it more interesting." When I asked about this seemingly inexhaustible group of guests whom her other friends did not know, she said, "Oh, whenever I meet someone interesting, I make a point of asking them. It's the easiest way to get to know people and get exposed to new ideas." For her, every day brings new experiences and new challenges, because she is looking for them.

She is a very wise woman. It is important to keep expanding one's social network. Old friends die or retire to another part of the country, and our children move away. There comes a time when family members of our own generation start disappearing. If you do not make an effort to bring new and younger people into your life, one morning you are going to wake up and discover you are the only one left.

This is when life becomes dull and boring. Humans are social animals. We need people in our lives if we are to thrive. We need someone to react to and who will react to us. We need stimulation if our brain is to function at its best.

It is not loneliness that is the problem, but the lack of stimulation. People think of older people as being lonely. It is true that death, divorce and circumstance have left many older women on their own. But lonely? Very seldom. Studies have shown, much to the researchers' surprise, that the least lonely groups of people are young children and older people. No one is immune to loneliness, but the over-sixty-fives score lower on all loneliness-measurement scales than other age groups. By and large, the older people get the more they enjoy solitude, which is quite different from loneliness. They have the inner resources that make being alone a pleasure. They welcome time alone as a chance to think, to plan, to read, to restore their energy, to do whatever they want to do.

Nevertheless, anyone of any age who does not have an active support network lacks the stimulation that keeps the spark of life glowing and the mind agile. The woman who finds herself too much alone can sink into mental and emotional apathy. This is a steep downward step on the road of life. Do not let yourself take it. Take action instead.

## A MATTER OF ATTITUDE

The best psychological tool I know for keeping one's life exciting and rewarding is to Act As If. Act As If you were thirty or forty or fifty, and your mind will respond. It is a matter of attitude. Make yourself open to people and ideas. Seek out activities that challenge your mind and imagination. The only way one can turn back the mind clock is to keep the brain busy, keep it working.

When I lecture on loneliness, I often talk about my Four Commandments, four ways to provide your brain with new and stimulating ideas and provide yourself with support networks. I recommend that people, no matter what their age, engage in activities from at least two of these Commandments. They are particularly valuable for older people whose social horizons are beginning to narrow.

1. *Join something.* A bridge club, the local conservation group, the historical society, a church organization, a women's

club, a quilting group, an exercise class, the garden club, the local political party organization, whatever.

2. *Learn something.* Take a course. An adult education course in computers, a course in topiary, art appreciation, watercolor painting, astronomy, Chinese, wine tasting. Pick a subject that interests you and learn more about it.

3. *Help with something.* There is so much that needs to be done in this world. Volunteers are needed in literally hundreds of areas. I don't suggest you take yourself off to mid-Africa to alleviate starvation, but you can help in your local hospital or library. You can help with such services as Meals on Wheels, driving the disabled to medical appointments. You can help raise money for the Red Cross, Planned Parenthood, cancer research, preserving the environment. The list is endless.

4. *Go someplace.* A change of environment may be the most rewarding and stimulating single thing you can do for yourself. I am not talking about going around the world. Just a trip to a place you have never been before. The American Association for Retired People offers hundreds of short and inexpensive trips that combine travel with education. Even a day away gives you a fresh perspective on life.

When you involve yourself in these activities, you are Acting As If you are full of curiosity and energy. As you pursue whichever ones you have chosen, you will soon become that energetic and involved woman without having to play-act. Your mental clock will start spinning backward, with all the stimulation you are giving those little gray cells. You will not only be living young, but thinking and acting young.

## FIGHTING AGE DISCRIMINATION

The older woman is wiser and more understanding, has far more experience, better judgment, greater capacity for joy and more time to devote to her own interests than in her younger years.

She may well need all these assets to cope with the age discrimination of our society.

There is a strong tendency for people, even members of one's own family, to treat older women as if they were less competent and less logical, less of a person than they really are. Unfortunately, some older people give in to this and begin to think that, "Well, perhaps I am not as competent and smart as I used to be." This is one of those self-destructive attitudes older women must fight. My mother did, right up to the very end. She was so determined to be self-sufficient that she would resist my sister's and my efforts to coddle her. "I'm just fine," she would say when I called her every day. "You'll have to excuse me now. I don't have time to talk, I have a date to play cards." Or she would be off to the movies or to visit a friend. In her eighties, there was always something she had to do. She was involved in life almost to the last day.

I was impressed by one woman who wrote me about her experience after retiring. She had been a high-school math teacher for forty years. "When I retired eighteen months ago at sixty-five," she wrote, "my daughter and son-in-law insisted that I come live with them where I would be 'safe.' I had some hesitations, but they were so loving and concerned that I agreed.

"It was a terrible mistake. I became a second-class citizen almost overnight. They treated me as if I were frail and incompetent. I was not welcome in the kitchen. 'Just sit down and relax,' my daughter would say. When I watched television in my room, they would insist that I join them downstairs, even though I pointed out that I preferred the programs on public television to the sitcoms they watched. They were very loving. It was just that we each had our own ways and interests.

"I moved out after three months, although they tried to convince me that I should not live on my own. I'm only sixty-six, for heaven's sake. There have been Presidents of the United States who were older than I am. They just had the idea that an older woman was not capable of looking after herself.

"I have a small apartment now where I can entertain my friends. And the school authorities recently asked me to set up an extracurricular math club for talented students. There is no money in it, but I can't tell you how stimulating it is to work with these youngsters.

"Why should I be considered a tottering old lady just because sixty-five is the mandatory retirement age in our school system? I look forward to another quarter-century of life and I intend to stay busy and involved."

This woman refused to be pushed into premature old age by social discrimination, even though it was lovingly and kindly motivated. She was wise enough to fight for her life.

Society fosters the idea that the older person becomes less mentally competent, less creative, less productive. Of course, in cases of certain illnesses, such as Alzheimer's disease, all this may be true, but the older woman in good health is competent and creative and productive.

As for memory, it continues with use and depreciates with disuse like any other skill. In fact, it tends to become more accurate with age, although the process is somewhat slower. Two groups, one aged thirty-five to forty-five and the other sixty-five to seventy-six, were asked to memorize a nonsense paragraph and then repeat it aloud to a researcher as part of a study at the University of Michigan. The members of the older group took longer to memorize the paragraph than those in the younger one, but they repeated it more accurately.

The best way to fight these discriminatory beliefs about age is through attitude. You can demonstrate that they are false by staying active, by being open to new ideas and activities, keeping involved with people. This is not just my opinion, it has been established by many studies, both physical and psychological.

Attitude is everything. If you give in passively, this self-destructive attitude will turn you old overnight. If you think of yourself as vital, strong, involved and interesting, you will live young and enjoy every minute of it.

There is a psychological technique that will help you establish the right attitude and armor you against age discrimination. It is a very short variation of the Basic Diagnostic List. No matter whether you are fifty-five or seventy-five or eighty-five, I recommend making one of these lists every six months. This variation of the Basic Diagnostic List is designed to help you set goals.

| My Goals | How to Achieve Goal |
|----------|---------------------|
| 1. | 1. |
| 2. | 2. |
| 3. | 3. |

This is all there is to it. Put down what you consider the three goals that you would like most to achieve and how you could go about achieving them. Then spend some time thinking about which goal is most important to you. It does not need to be an earth-shaking goal. Perhaps you think you would like to see a whale. Or go to Las Vegas and hit the slot machines. But once you have chosen your goal, go for it.

The happiest and most vital people are those who have goals, but one goal is not enough. You need a constant supply of new goals. This is because every time you attain a goal, you are happy, but only for a time. Then you have to set yourself a new one.

Ronald Inglehart of the University of Michigan and Jacques-René Rabier of the Commission of the European Communities, who are researching the sources of happiness, explain it this way. Suppose you are lost in the desert and are close to dying of thirst. Finally you reach an oasis with water. You dance for joy. But, the researchers ask, would that oasis and its water make you as happy a week later? Of course not. You would take it for granted and start to worry about when someone would come to rescue you. When they do, you will fall on their necks with relief and be ecstatically happy. But when you get back to civilization, you will need another goal if you are to achieve happiness again.

By redoing the variation of the Diagnostic List every six months, you will have a never-ending supply of goals. A woman who has a support network, is involved in at least two of the Four Commandment activities, and who has goals for the future is the best argument against age discrimination one could want.

## FEARS OF THE FUTURE

No matter how upbeat your attitude, there is always a time when worries descend like a flock of vultures. You become distressed. The quality of your life goes downhill. You are living old instead of living young.

When this happens, get to work on a Worst-Case Scenario. Write down all your fears—illness, dependency, money problems, everything. After you have given this list of fears some thought, write down the very worst that could happen in each instance. Perhaps you fear falling and breaking a leg or a hip. What is the very worst that could happen if you did? What changes in your life would it involve? What is it you are most afraid of?

This has two benefits. First, it makes you face the worst and think about how to cope with it. Second, by facing your fears, they become less frightening. It is the unknown that scares us.

When you have completed your Scenario, Previsualize each of your fears. What would happen? Is that really the way it would work out? Might there be another solution? Try to visualize alternative ways to handle whichever fear you are concentrating on.

Once you start visualizing what it would mean to spend your life in a wheelchair or to move to an apartment or a retirement home or what inflation is going to do to your income, you have already began to change your attitude. You are thinking solutions. The worst is no longer as scary. You can handle it.

Your next move is to decide which of these terrors is really likely to happen. Bad things do happen, but not every terrible thing you can think of is going to happen to you. Zero in on the two or three that might just possibly lie in store for you and think them through. How will you stay involved and active, if such and such should happen? How will you stay in touch with friends? What will you be able to afford? Once you have Previsualized what kind of life-change each happening will entail, start thinking about ways you might prevent your fear from coming true.

If you turn back your biological clock with exercise and a healthy diet, for instance, you may never have to see the inside of a nursing home. If you sell your house and rent an apartment, your money may be less likely to run out.

Write everything down and then file the whole thing away and forget it for six months. Review your Worst-Case Scenario twice a year. You will probably come up with new and better solutions, because the review forces you to think constructively. This is one of the keys to turning back the brain clock. The more you use your mind imaginatively and constructively, the sharper it stays.

## LIVING YOUNG

A positive attitude cannot turn back the chronological clock, but it can turn back the body clock and give you more strength, more energy, better health and possibly add years to your life. A negative attitude can hasten the onset of illness, weakness and other debilities.

A positive attitude cannot make you more intelligent, but it can turn back the brain clock and substitute optimism, goals and involvement for the dreary passivity, complaints and discontent that many associate with old age. A negative attitude will dull your brain and take the joy out of this last chapter of life.

Turning back your biological and mental clocks will improve the quality of your life beyond belief. It is up to you. Will you turn them back and live young? Why not? You will be giving yourself a wonderful gift—a better and possibly longer life.

*Epilogue*

# SUMMING UP

## Tools for a Lifetime

YOU NOW HAVE your own Psychological Tool
techniques that you can use to transform undesi
or attitudes into more desirable ones, to help n
decisions and to solve all kinds of personal prob
guide your thoughts and behavior into construct
tive channels.

I devised these tools, which are based on esta
logical precepts, to help people help themselves
best of their worst. Their use is by no means
traits and attitudes discussed in the preceding ch
use them to alter almost any behavior that is blc
attaining your potential. These tools can also be
your own special needs.

I have included several variations of the Li
Conditioning techniques in these chapters, but t
ations are limitless. Now that you understand
works, you can customize it to apply to any tr
fine-tune or decision that you must make. These
you well all your life long.

They are not magic, but I believe you will fi
miraculously effective in transforming undesiral
sets. They can help you become the person you
better. Let me know how you do.

that many associate with old age. A negative attitude will dull your brain and take the joy out of this last chapter of life.

Turning back your biological and mental clocks will improve the quality of your life beyond belief. It is up to you. Will you turn them back and live young? Why not? You will be giving yourself a wonderful gift—a better and possibly longer life.

*Epilogue*

# SUMMING UP

---

## Tools for a Lifetime

---

YOU NOW HAVE your own Psychological Tool Kit containing techniques that you can use to transform undesirable behaviors or attitudes into more desirable ones, to help make important decisions and to solve all kinds of personal problems. They will guide your thoughts and behavior into constructive and productive channels.

I devised these tools, which are based on established psychological precepts, to help people help themselves by making the best of their worst. Their use is by no means confined to the traits and attitudes discussed in the preceding chapters. You can use them to alter almost any behavior that is blocking you from attaining your potential. These tools can also be modified to fit your own special needs.

I have included several variations of the List and Operant Conditioning techniques in these chapters, but the possible variations are limitless. Now that you understand how each tool works, you can customize it to apply to any trait you want to fine-tune or decision that you must make. These tools will serve you well all your life long.

They are not magic, but I believe you will find them almost miraculously effective in transforming undesirable traits into assets. They can help you become the person you really are—only better. Let me know how you do.